International Trade, Wage Inequality
and the Developing Economy

Contributions to Economics

http://www.springer.de/cgi-bin/search_book.pl?series=1262

Sugata Marjit
Rajat Acharyya

International Trade, Wage Inequality and the Developing Economy

A General Equilibrium Approach

With 19 Figures
and 15 Tables

Physica-Verlag

A Springer-Verlag Company

331.22
M32i

Series Editors
Werner A. Müller
Martina Bihn

Authors

Prof. Sugata Marjit
Centre for Studies in Social Sciences
R1, Baishnabghata Patuli Township
Calcutta 700094 ₍ₐₖ₎
India
smarjit@hotmail.com

Dr. Rajat Acharyya
Department of Economics
Jadavpur University
Calcutta 700032
India
racharya@cal2.vsnl.net.in

ISSN 1431-1933
ISBN 3-7908-0031-7 Physica-Verlag Heidelberg New York

Cataloging-in-Publication Data applied for
A catalog record for this book is available from the Library of Congress.
Bibliographic information published by Die Deutsche Bibliothek
Die Deutsche Bibliothek lists this publication in the Deutsche Nationalbibliografie; detailed bibliographic
data is available in the Internet at <http://dnb.ddb.de>.

Physica-Verlag Heidelberg New York
a member of BertelsmannSpringer Science+Business Media GmbH

© Physica-Verlag Heidelberg 2003
Printed in Germany

The use of general descriptive names, registered names, trademarks, etc. in this publication does not imply,
even in the absence of a specific statement, that such names are exempt from the relevant protective laws and
regulations and therefore free for general use.

Softcover Design: Erich Kirchner, Heidelberg

SPIN 10909652   88/3130/DK-5 4 3 2 1 0 – Printed on acid-free and non-aging paper

For

Chitra Marjit, Baisakhi Marjit and Anima Debi

and

Ira and Sundari Mohan Acharyya

PREFACE

Globalization, as is popularly used, defines a process of integration with the rest-of-the world. Such integration is routed through increasing volume of foreign trade and investment. Major task of an economist is to work out the welfare implications of such a transformation both from the aggregative and distributive perspectives. With regard to the distributive effect, economists in the industrialized world have been worried over a noticeable empirical phenomenon that suggests a decline in the income of the unskilled labour and/or a decline in their employment relative to the more skilled segment of the workforce. This has happened in the US and in Europe over the last twenty years and has roughly coincided with the buoyant phase of international trade and investment. The scenario in the developing countries is not different either. Except for a few East Asian countries, the general trend has been an increase in the ratio of skilled to unskilled wages.

However, the overwhelming empirical research, delving into the causation between freer trade and wage inequality, has not been supplemented by well-constructed and relevant theoretical analyses particularly from the developing country perspective. As a consequence, the gulf between conventional wisdom gained from the theory and empirical finding has been widened further. An apathy towards having a closer look at the labour markets of the developing countries and a casual treatment of the trade theory, ignoring the possibilities that lie underneath the surface, means committing the theory to conclusions which are only artifacts of weak theorization. This is what this book tries to avoid and for this purpose we suggest models that can be used in the applied work instead of the straightjacket application of the Stolper-Samuelson result. The empirical methodology, which illuminates our view regarding trade and wage inequality, is extremely difficult to implement in an aggregative study because one has to control for many variables that determine the degree of inequality. Controlling for other explanatory factors also means that one is more or less certain about the mechanism, which determines the nature of such partial dependence of inequality on trade and investment. Exploring such a mechanism rigorously is what we set out for in this book. It has to do with predicting the likely outcomes of liberalizing trade if one is concerned with the real income of the poor workers, in economies which exhibit large agricultural sectors, pockets of economic sophistication, possibly dualism, large informal labour markets, non-traded activities, capital constraints etc.

Such proliferation of concerns sounds far too complex to experiment within a general equilibrium framework. But as we argue, between the vintage two-sector Heckscher-Ohlin structure and a multi-sector analytically unsolvable general equilibrium model lies the possibility of constructing something meaningful, of course more transparent to people who appreciate theory, but not less interesting to a wide range of economists. We cater to the view that the urge for having new models to explain facts can easily undermine our inability to appreciate the hidden advantage of using conventional models or their variants. Unfortunately, their limits are kept under-explored and hence their understanding remains incomplete. It is no wonder that the silver jubilee of issue of the Journal of International Economics (2000) convincingly makes use of the Heckscher-Ohlin-Samuelson models to reflect upon the burning issues even after gradual and intense development of competing frameworks over the last twenty years.

A major purpose of this book is to make senior undergraduates and postgraduate students aware of the usefulness of simple general equilibrium models. The material contained can indeed be a part of a course on trade and development as it covers a wide range of issues and gives a comprehensive, though critical, picture of the existing literature. In fact, these chapters in some form or the other have been taught and/or discussed in seminars and special lectures by at least one of us in Monash University in Australia; Erasmus University at Rotterdam, University of Konstanz, University of Munich, University of Innsbruck and Copenhagen Business School in Europe; Chinese and City Universities of Hong Kong; Presidency College, Jadavpur University, Indian Statistical Institute (Calcutta, Delhi), Indira Gandhi Institute of Development Research (Mumbai), University of Bombay (Mumbai), Centre for Studies in Social Sciences, Calcutta, Calcutta University, SNDT Women University (Mumbai), Jawaharlal Nehru University and Rabindrabharati University in India; and Columbia University, Cornell University, Northern Illinois University, Pennsylvania State University, SUNY at Albany and Buffalo, University of Florida, Gainesville, University of Pittsburgh and University of Rochester in USA.

Several teachers, friends and colleagues have helped us over the last twenty years with the understanding of the general equilibrium theories and hence with the gradual development of the book. In particular, we would like to thank Max Albert, Kaushik Basu, Hamid Beladi, Eric Bond, Udo Broll, James Cassing, Ajit Chowdhury, Satya P. Das, Dietrich Fausten, Robert C. Feenstra, Ronald Findlay, Eric Fisher, Manas Ranjan Gupta, Arye Hillman, M. Ali Khan, Arup Mallik, Tapan Mitra, Anjan Mukherjee, Michiro Ohyama, Alok Ray, Kalyan K. Sanyal, Abhirup Sarkar, Partha Sen, Sarbajit Sengupta, Richard Snape, J.M. Viaene, H.J. Vosgerau, Henry Wan (Jr.), Makato Yano and Eden Yu. Our greatest intellectual debt is to Ronald W. Jones for shaping our interest in trade theory. We are also grateful to him for detailed comments on an earlier draft of the manuscript. Finally, we would like to thank our students for their interest in our courses and insightful queries that have made us think deeper and clean up our intuitive arguments.

November 2002   S. Marjit
                                                                R. Acharyya

CONTENTS

1 INTRODUCTION

The imagined boundary of the world is getting smaller every day and that too at a very rapid pace. The volume of world trade and communications has grown phenomenally over the recent years. Physical and policy barriers to trade and investment are being systematically abolished, thanks to the increasing use of web based contacts and coordinated process of liberalization through the institutions such as the WTO. The earlier stance of protected industrialization has given way to deregulation and reform in the developing nations with a switch towards free international trade and foreign investment. At times it is hard to argue against the policies that put emphasis on the national welfare as opposed to global welfare, policies that provide the government with power to redistribute, enforce equity and correct negative externalities. But the historical evidence so far has not been in favour of socialistic and closed economies. For example, it is now well known that the Indian economy somehow did not respond to the maze of regulations and controls. The so called public sector has not performed well and most importantly the condition of the bottom 30 percent of the population has not changed much over the long phase of planned development. The Russian debacle along with the political turn around in the Eastern Europe also reflected the need for experimentation of a different kind. However, the Chinese case stands out as a reasonable success story of reform without the sacrifice of the basic tenets of socialism.

A question that lurks behind the potential success of international trade or greater integration of the world, has to do with the internal distribution of such gains. The story of the North-South divide and the issue of unequal exchange in the process of international trade has taken a back seat because some of the so-called Southern countries, as they were defined in the 1960s and 70s, have done remarkably well in the trade front. The success story of the East and South East Asia, notwithstanding the financial crisis that hit the region a few years back, points towards the positive role of trade in economic prosperity. It is difficult to convince someone of the hypothesis that engaging in international trade is potentially harmful for a poor economy. But gains from trade are not evenly distributed within an economy. Politically it becomes very difficult to tax the gainers and bribe the losers, and therefore to generate a national consensus on liberal trade policies. However, such maldistribution may not necessarily aggravate the existing distributional pattern. Typically the exports are made out of the relatively abundant factor available within the country. Prior to trade, scarce factors will be priced higher than the abundant factors, relatively speaking. As trade opens up, the relative price of the abundant factors will have a tendency to go up. This suggests that trade will be equalizing in some sense. However, innocence of such logic falls flat on its face because of two reasons.

First, the gap between the average income of the scarce and the abundant factor can be very high and trade may further widen the gap. For example, it is taken for granted that the USA and Europe are relatively well endowed with skilled labour compared to the developing countries. Trade, by encouraging exports of the skilled intensive goods, should increase the skilled wage relative to the unskilled wage. Although the wage gap between the abundant and the scarce factor is moving towards the abundant factor, such a move is increasing the degree of inequality as the unskilled workers get less than their skilled counterpart. If protection makes the unskilled better off, liberal trade policies will make them worse off. Such a phenomenon has triggered off heated debates among trade and labor economists on both sides of the Atlantic. Casual as well as rigorous empirical observations reveal that for the US economy skilled - unskilled wage gap has been increasing along with the gradual opening up of the US economy. A similar fate has affected the labor market in Europe as well with increasing magnitude of unemployment among the unskilled. Such a course of events is politically disturbing as it brings along vehement lobbying against free trade, frequent appeals for anti-dumping and slogans against labour standards in the poor countries.

Second, the problem of free trade and wage-gap or income inequality assumes further significance in the light of the fact that the developing countries, in spite of being endowed with a huge supply of unskilled labour may not be able to reduce inequality through trade. Conventional wisdom, however, suggests otherwise. Since the relatively abundant factor, which generates exportables, is labour with little or no skill, greater export growth will increase their income relative to the factors employed in the import competing sector. Hence a more open trade regime should bring down inequality in the South. Such a typical Heckscher-Ohlin conjecture or the Stolper-Samuelson type outcome should be the case and therefore even if the unskilled is up with arms in the North, their brothers in the South should welcome the process of free trade. This line of arguments requires several qualifications which we attempt in various chapters of the book. Except for a few cases, all the evidence available so far indicates that the degree of wage inequality in the South is on the rise as well. Our starting query has to do with the issue of this symmetric widening of the wage gap in the developed as well as developing countries. While the standard 2x2 trade models cannot explain such a phenomenon, variants of it can. We stick to the conventional methodology to reflect on this stylized fact before we enter the more complex terrain of specific issues affecting the conditions of labour in the developing countries.

For the labour rich poor economies, it is important that one deals explicitly with the consequence of international integration on the welfare of labour, relative or absolute. This has to specify the avenues through which the effects of trade and investment impact on the condition of the workers. The existing theoretical structures developed mostly in the context of the labor and commodity markets in the West do not suit the discussion of such issues in the developing countries. Moreover, the conventional models of trade and income distribution fail to yield the right result when the structure of trade is complex, when the process of commodity market and factor market interaction can not be captured in terms of the standard 2x2 framework and when initial distribution of resources matter a lot in determining the equilibrium outcome.

One way to justify the present work is to suggest that the implications of a more open trade and investment regime have to be analyzed in terms of frameworks which explicitly take into account the structural features of labour markets in the LDCs. The idea of a segmented labour market is extremely relevant here since the majority of workers in the developing countries are employed in the informal or unorganized sector of the economy. It is a widely observed characteristic of the entire developing world. The interaction between the formal and the informal labour markets provides an interesting twist to the standard neoclassical general equilibrium models and lead to interesting relationship between commodity and factor prices. In fact the informal segment can accommodate voluntary and involuntary employment at the same time and trade reform tends to affect their incentives in different ways. We bring this aspect into the standard models of trade and production and we hope that it generates sufficient testable hypotheses for subsequent empirical work which is not pursued explicitly in this book. The specific set of analytical models developed for the purpose is rare and not published before. While we feel that a rich body of theoretical literature has provided the building block for the empirical analyses of trade and inequality, models that can address specifically the problem of the developing nations are not available to that extent at least within a properly collated format. As we shall argue in the book, interpreting empirical observations in 1990s in terms of the textbook models developed in the 60s is an insult to trade and general equilibrium theory. This has characterized whatever little empirical work there is on trade and inequality in developing countries. The basic idea of Stolper-Samuelson or the Specific-Factor models can be extended quite realistically to reflect on the issue of wage inequality in the developing country. But as we shall argue, such extensions must be done with an eye to the existing economic environment of the developing world. Typically, extending the 2x2 models to higher dimensions yield non-robust results and often reflect uninteresting academic exercise. But thanks to some recent developments in this field, we do have a range of useful models that are interesting, robust and relevant for the world around us. In a way our results reconfirm the usefulness of the simple general equilibrium models.

One should make amends by saying that there is a voluminous literature on trade and unemployment focusing particularly the concern of the developing countries and therefore our work should not ignore the existence of such a huge literature. In fact it does not. We propose to summarize those issues in terms of models which can be taught as a part of a course in trade and development. We attempt to inject a contemporary flavour into these models and draw from existing empirical work to make these models fit more to the prevailing conditions of the developing markets. These in turn are related to the general theme of trade and inequality.

This book is essentially a theoretical one which uses a large number of simply structured general equilibrium models to reflect on the particular cases of concern. However, it makes an attempt to gather all the secondary information available so far on openness and inequality in the developing world. We take recourse to a large number of papers to report their findings, discuss them and organize them according to our analytical need. There are a few first hand statistical information gathered in the Indian context to make our theoretical effort more convincing and appealing to the readers. Models constructed in the book are based on assumptions generally acceptable to people who are aware of the economic environment of the poor countries.

As a parting remark, before we go into the summary of the chapters, we would like to admit our inability to capture several other dimensions of inequality related to gender, literacy and other social opportunities in terms of the framework developed. Wage-gap or differences in real income levels have been our main concern because we respect the tradition of trade and general equilibrium theory. Moreover, the direct impact of an open trade and investment regime is felt on labour income in the traded and non-traded sectors. We agree that the severity of adverse shocks depends on the role of the state and the distributive system, formal as well as informal. At a deeper plane the so-called globalizing process tends to have a fundamental impact on the social philosophy of poor protected nation-states. It is futile to stretch the boundaries of economics as a discipline to account for such transformations. While we are aware of the importance of such consequence, we still feel that most visible manifestation of such a process, that affects the general population, takes place through short run adjustments in the levels of income and such adjustments are definitely matters of serious concern. Also our purpose is to extend the horizon of the applicability of simple general equilibrium models, to make them more acceptable to the students and researchers of trade and development. International trade, labour and wage inequality is an interesting topic to drive home our point. As the chapters would reveal, we provide a plethora of workable models to understand the relationship between trade, employment and the wage-gap. We do not cater to the view that there is a single unifying structure that should answer all our queries. Although the broad framework within which such models are constructed (or reconstructed), happens to be the same, variations in models are needed to capture specific circumstances of concern.

The book has been divided into four parts. Part I puts together the trends in employment of unskilled labour and in the wage-gap between the skilled and unskilled workers in the US, Europe, Asia and Latin-America. The debate over the plausible causes underlying the observed widening of the wage gap is summarized next.

Part II investigates the possible theoretical explanations for the *symmetric* movements in relative wages across the trading nations. In Chapter 3 we examine how far the predictions of the standard 2x2 Heckscher-Ohlin-Samuelson (HOS) model and its Specific-Factor variants, regarding wage movements in the trading nations, differ from the facts. The next two Chapters provide a few extensions of these basic theoretical structures that produce results almost similar to what has been observed. First is the case of fewer domestic factors of production than the commodities forcing the trading economies to specialize only in a few and importing the rest from others. As we spell out in Chapter 4, under such circumstances one should focus on the *local* factor intensity of goods that may differ across the countries depending on the significantly different endowment patterns and thus form the basis of the symmetric wage movements despite asymmetric price changes following opening up of trade among themselves. This is similar to the concept of local factor abundance used by Donald Davis to explain asymmetric wage movements across the Southern or the developing countries. Second is the role of a fixed unskilled money wage in a situation where traded goods are less in number than the domestic factors of production. In Chapter 5 we talk about the third possibility by allowing for input trade and capital mobility, two important features of the North-South trade, to examine how far these can explain the observed symmetric wage movements.

Part III of the book concentrates on the impact of trade and investment liberalization on organized sector employment. We put together some of our earlier work in this direction as well as a few from the existing literature both in the context of dual-economy and general equilibrium models. Though these analyses do not address how trade affects the informal sectors that provide a significant proportion of total employment in the developing countries, they are useful in understanding how trade might displace labour from the organized sectors and push them to the unsecured informal markets.

In the three chapters in Part IV we develop models relevant for the developing countries to reconcile the trade induced widening of wage-gap with unskilled labour intensive exports. Chapter 7, the first in the line, focuses on the non-Harris-Todaro type dual economy characterization of the developing countries. Our primary focus here is on role of the bimodal comparative advantage of a few Southern countries such as India and China as reflected in their diversified trade patterns in terms of the skill-intensity of exports, and on the complementarity between such exports. Another typical feature of North-South trade is that of specialization in parts rather than in finished products wherever technology permits such fragmentation. Due to capital scarcity in the developing countries, it is much easier for them to produce and export fragments or assemble fragments. We show that such fragmentation and the issue of wage inequality is intertwined.

Segmented input markets are typical feature of many developing country. The formal unskilled labour markets with minimum wage laws and job security coexist with the unorganized sectors where the money wage varies with the changes in demand for and supply of unskilled labour. These are the sectors where unskilled labour is hired and fired as and when necessary. The wages are low compared to those in the formal sectors that are often unionized. Production of non-traded goods is another important feature. It is well known by now that existence of such goods significantly alters many of the standard results. In Chapter 8 we bring out the implications of such structural characteristics specific to the labour markets in poor countries.

There is scattered evidence of *asymmetric* changes in relative wages of workers with different levels of skills. In Chapter 9 we trace out the possible explanations in terms of a general equilibrium model with a continuum of skills. An overpowering consequence of globalization for the developing countries is its impact on the internal demand for and supply of skill. Increasing trade and investment requires specialized skills which may be in short supply in a developing country. Hence, one would expect that with the expansion of trade, the process of skill formation would also get a natural boost increasing the knowledge base of the economy which in turn will have growth enhancing effects. The major part of Chapter 9 is devoted to discuss this process of skill formation and its implications on the wage inequality. Such an analysis essentially supplements the theoretical framework of the earlier chapters.

I

EVIDENCE AND THE DEBATE

2 WAGES AND EMPLOYMENT

2.1 Country Experiences

Despite asymmetries in the extent of changes in relative wages of skilled and unskilled workers, the experiences of the high, middle and low income countries are more or less similar. Except for the East Asian countries, the general trend has been an increase in the ratio of skilled to unskilled wages, i.e., a widening wage-gap between skilled and unskilled workers, in most part of the globe since 1970s [Wood (1997)]. In Europe, where national institutions have a particularly strong influence on wage settings, the deterioration of the relative position of relatively unskilled workers is reflected in rising unemployment of the unskilled. Though concerns for widening wage-gap have been rather recent, employment aspect has always held the centre-stage in evaluating success and continuation of trade policies. It is such concerns, particularly the disemployment effect, that in many instances policy reversals are in fact observed. For example, during 1965-66 in Israel the liberalization programmes were deferred whereas Spain partially reversed its policies in its third episode of liberalization during 1977-80.

This chapter summarizes the developed and the developing country experiences regarding such changes in the relative wages and employment and their association with trade dependence or openness of the country as measured by the volume of trade as a proportion of gross domestic product (GDP).

2.2.1 The US Experience after the 1970s

Social concern for the condition of working class in the US did not take the centre-stage in the 1960s and 1970s simply because the ratio of unskilled to skilled wage showed gradual improvements during that period. Over the 1970s, for example, although the US economy became considerably open, the premium earned by educated workers actually declined. The situation has changed drastically from the late 1970s as the real wages have stagnated and relative wages have become more dispersed. These have been accompanied by a dramatic increase in inequality of earnings based on education, experience and occupation. For example, as observed by Bound and Johnson (1992), the ratio of the average wage of a college graduate to the average wage of a high school graduate rose by 15 percent.

Table 2.1, reproduced from Leamer (2000), reports manufacturing earnings of each education group relative to earnings of college graduates, normalized to one in 1971. It is evident that, in manufacturing, there has been steady and persistent widening of earnings between college graduates and high-school (HS) dropouts since the 1971. The 1994 share of HS dropouts compared with college graduates was only 15 percent of its 1971 level. For the high-school graduates, on the other hand, the situation improved during the first half of the 1970s, but since then deteriorated steadily.

Such a dramatic turnaround in the relative wages and the consequent relative impoverishment of the unskilled workers has triggered heated discussions and debates on the causes of these changes. The current state of the controversies has been nicely summarized in Jones and Engerman (1996). Essentially, two sets of issues have become triumphant in this debate: Trade-related and technology-related. We will return to this later.

Table 2.1

The US Experience: Earnings Relative to College Graduates

Year	HS dropouts	HS graduates	Some college
1971	1.00	1.00	1.00
1972	0.95	1.11	0.97
1973	0.91	1.11	1.06
1974	0.82	1.08	1.05
1975	0.73	1.00	1.01
1976	0.69	1.01	1.07
1977	0.68	1.02	1.05
1978	0.61	0.98	1.01
1979	0.55	0.94	1.01
1980	0.48	0.90	0.99
1981	0.46	0.89	0.99
1982	0.39	0.81	0.92
1983	0.31	0.73	0.85
1984	0.29	0.69	0.80
1985	0.26	0.68	0.79
1986	0.25	0.65	0.83
1987	0.23	0.61	0.81
1988	0.23	0.64	0.81
1989	0.23	0.64	0.85
1990	0.20	0.62	0.84
1991	0.19	0.58	0.84
1992	0.18	0.55	0.97
1993	0.15	0.50	0.98
1994	0.15	0.48	1.00

Source: Leamer (2000).

2.1.2 The European Wage and Employment Performance

The case of Europe is altogether different. With the national institutions having a strong influence on wage setting there, the important issue is the degree to which such institutional and regulatory forces repressed wage adjustments and instead raised unemployment. The strongest bastion of the European Monetary Union (EMU), Germany, has exhibited significant unemployment rates and the root cause has often been cited to be rigid labour laws and social safety-net contributions of the employer. Table 2.2 shows the changes in the rate of unemployment in some European countries during 1991-98. Except Netherlands and the UK in the later half of the period, all the countries have experienced growing unemployment rates. In Sweden, the unemployment rate has doubled from the lowest rate of 3 percent among these countries in 1991. Similar had been the case in Finland and in Portugal in the first half of 1990s.

Table 2.2

Unemployment in Selected European Countries: 1991-1998
(% of Total Labour Force)

	1991	1995	1998
Finland	6.60	15.20	11.30
France	9.40	11.60	11.80
Germany	6.60	10.10	9.70
Greece	7.70	10.00	10.30
Netherlands	7.00	7.10	4.40
Portugal	4.10	7.10	5.00
Spain	16.40	22.93	18.82
Sweden	3.00	7.70	6.50
United Kingdom	8.40	8.60	6.10

Source: World Development Indicator 2001, CD-ROM.

Regarding wages, Lawrence (1994) has reported that between 1978 and 1988, the ratio of manual to non-manual wages fell by 8.1 percent in Germany and by 3 percent in Italy whereas they actually increased in Belgium and Denmark. According to the OECD Employment Outlook (1993), on the other hand, there was a substantial increase in the ratio of earnings of the highest to lowest percentiles in the UK. Similar was the findings of Katz, Loveman and Blanchflower (1992).

Just like the US, in Europe too international trade has been conceived as the major source of these poor labour market performances. As Lawrence (1994) points out, in the European debate about freer trade with Eastern Europe and Asia, "concerns have been raised not simply about low wages but about social dumping, i.e., the downwards competitive pressures that are allegedly placed on labour standards as a result of trade". Moreover, the inclusion of low-wage countries such as Spain, Portugal and Greece into the European Union has worsened the scenario through relocation of firms to these countries. Shift of the Hoover Corporation from France to Scotland, attracted by both lower wage costs and lower labour standards, is a glaring example.

2.1.3 The Widening Wage-Gap in Latin-America

The studies by Robbins covering Chile, Colombia, Costa Rica, Mexico and Uruguay, reveal widening of the skill differentials in wages (by the level of education) in almost all these countries contrary to the conventional wisdom. The indices for wages, the weighted averages across sex and experience, and the ratio of wage of workers with secondary level education to that of workers with primary level of education as reported by Robbins are clear indication of the widening wage-gap phenomenon. Table 2.3 reports the movement in the wage ratio in these countries.

Table 2.3
Relative Wages: The Latin-American Case

Country	(Secondary/Primary)	
	1976	1989
Chile	2.08	2.11
Costa Rica	1.95	1.61
Colombia	2.33	1.62
Mexico	1.41	1.46
Uruguay	1.60	1.62

Source: Robbins (1995a).

Of late, Pederson (1998) corroborates findings of Robbins for Chile by reporting about a study which shows that over the 1980s the wage of the university graduates relative to that of the high school graduates went up by 56 percent. On the contrary, however, Meller (1998) finds the White-Blue wage differentials going down between 1984 and 1992.

In an interesting piece of study Beyer, et. al. (1999) give an account of the distribution of labour income of Chilean households according to the education level of the head of the family. Table 2.4 summarizes their findings. The average labour income of a university graduate in 1960 was more than double that of the head of the household with only secondary education. By 1996, it was 3.3 times. This trend has been stronger among the younger age groups. But the gap between average labour income of those completing secondary education and those who only finish primary education, among 25 -35 year old, has narrowed down. Thus, movement in relative wages of different skill or education groups has been asymmetric.

Table 2.4
Ratio of Average Labour Income Received by Heads of Households
According to Education Level and Age in Chile

	1960	1970	1980	1990	1996
University/Secondary education					
25 to 35	2.1	2.2	2.4	4.2	4.0
36 to 50	2.3	2.4	2.6	3.3	3.2
Over 50	2.3	2.0	2.3	3.1	2.7
Total	2.2	2.3	2.4	3.6	3.3
University/Primary education					
25 to 35	4.1	4.5	4.8	7.0	5.1
36 to 50	5.5	5.4	6.5	7.1	5.6
Over 50	6.0	4.4	6.4	8.1	6.1
Total	5.1	4.9	5.7	7.2	5.6
Secondary /Primary education					
25 to 35	2.0	2.1	2.1	1.7	1.3
36 to 50	2.4	2.2	2.5	2.1	1.8
Over 50	2.6	2.2	2.8	2.6	2.3
Total	2.3	2.2	2.4	2.0	1.7

Source : As reported in Beyer et. al. (1999)

2.1.4 East Asia: A Mixed Experience

For East Asia the empirical findings available so far point towards a mixed experience. The wage-gap declined in Korea and Taiwan during the 1960s and in Singapore during 1970s. In all these three cases, according to Wood (1997), changes in the trade regime were partly responsible[1].

---

[1] The major problem with the empirical exercise, as pointed out by Wood (1997), is that the data on the relative wages contains gaps and deficiencies. Moreover, while finding the relationship between trade and wage-gap, only a few analyses have attempted to control for the internal influences on the movement of relative wages.

Similar to the experience of the three tigers, Robbins (1994a) finds persistent compression of wage differentials by the level of education in Malaysia from 1973-1989, particularly between university graduates and educated workers. This went on in the early 1990s with the skilled and semi-skilled blue-collar workers in the manufacturing sector gaining relative to others. However, despite the increasing openness from a high initial level of 70 percent in 1970 to nearly 100 percent in 1983 and then to 150 percent by 1992, and shift in demand in favour of less-skilled workers within industries because of trade-related changes in product mix, Robbins (1994a) denies the role of trade openness in such decline in wage-gap. The relative growth in the number of highly educated workers is what he ascribed as the primary factor instead.

The case of Philippines is less transparent during its modest liberalization episode (1978-88). Skill differentials in wages widened during severe recession in 1982-86, but then narrowed down again [Robbins (1994b)]. On the other hand, the wage-gap has widened in Hong Kong more or less consistently, which according to Wood (1997) may have been largely due to the substantial increase in the relative supply of unskilled labour instead of trade policy change.

Though there has been no study on the wage-gap in China, the survey by the State Statistical Bureau in 1999 reveals growing income inequality there with the emergence of a very rich population. In just over 10 years, China has gone from being an egalitarian country to one with substantial income inequality. The wealthiest 10 percent of the urban population earn at least 30,000 Yuan a year that is more than four times of the urban average of 6,300 yuan and more than 13 times of the rural average of 2,250 yuan. These are mostly the skilled people with greater initiative to earn the rewards offered by the market. At the same time over a million urban workers have lost their jobs and are living on survival allowances of 100 - 200 yuan a month. Similar concern has been echoed in *China Investigation Report 2000-2001 : Studies of Contradictions Within the People Under New Conditions*, compiled by the Department of Organization Research Group of the Communist Party Central Committee. The report recognizes that the fast-growing wage-gaps between urban and rural people and within the urban population is driven by the planned opening up of markets to foreign trade and investment, which may impede reform programmes and accession to the WTO.

2.1.5   South Asia: Widening Wage-Gap with Rising Employment?

Though any comprehensive empirical study is yet to come by, some casual empiricism, however, points to a widening wage-gap in South Asia including India. The impact of the so-called globalization in this region is studied from a broader perspective of growth and poverty by Khan (1998a) and Tendulkar et. al. (1996). Khan (1998a) finds that the process of expansion in foreign trade and investment in South Asian countries is consistent with rising incidence of poverty in these nations. Typically, if poverty is really on the rise then it must worsen the inequality situation.

The experience of Bangladesh is somewhat mixed. Whatever little evidence is available indicates that during 1991-92 the overall skilled-unskilled wage ratio widened marginally from 2.56 to 2.62, but that for the female workers declined significantly from 1.94 to 1.82 (Yearbook of Labour Statistics, 1999). However, rapid export growth in the first half of the 1990s was accompanied by rising inequality. The Gini coefficient increased from 26 to 31 between 1992 and 1996. For Sri Lanka, on the other hand, there is clear evidence of widening wage-gap during 1977-1985 (see Table 2.5). Though the gap between minimum wages for the skilled and unskilled workers was more or less stable, differentials in actual earnings increased substantially.

Table 2.5
Ratio of Skilled to Unskilled Rates in Sri Lanka

	Minimum Wage	Monthly Earnings
1977	1.21	1.17
1980	1.14	1.26
1981	1.13	1.44
1983	1.12	1.39
1985	1.10	1.42

Source: Rodrigo (1988).

Although no systematic study on wage-dispersion across skill or education level in India is available, of late Shariff and Gumber (1999) put forward some evidence regarding growing wage inequality in some of the sectors in the post-reform periods (Table 2.6). The wage-gap between the graduate and non-literate has widened significantly in transport & storage, agriculture and in services. On the other hand, the gap between graduate and workers with secondary-level education has widened in almost all the sectors except electricity, construction and trade. There has, however, been an asymmetric change in the relative wages across different skill categories in the manufacturing sector which deserve attention. Whereas the wage-gap between graduates and secondary-level educated workers has widened, the position of the non-literates relative to the graduates has vastly improved during the same period. This is somewhat similar to the Chilean experience.

More systematic data is, on the other hand, available for employment growth in South Asia. Dev (2000) provides a detailed account of such employment changes.

Table 2.7 shows that for Pakistan the growth rate of aggregate employment has registered a decline over the period 1986-93 compared to the first half of the 1980s, whereas for Sri Lanka it has increased quite remarkably over the same period. India too has recorded substantial increase in growth rate of employment. More importantly, in both India and Sri Lanka such growth rates have been well above the growth rates of the workforce indicating therefore a decline in the overall unemployment during 1986-93. Such changes are in striking contrast to rising unemployment in these countries during 1981-85 (see columns 2 and 4). For Pakistan, on the other hand, the trend of rising unemployment continues.

Table 2.6

Change in Wage Ratio in India by Sector

Sectors	Graduate/Secondary		Graduate/Non-literate	
	1987-88	1993-94	1987-88	1993-94
1. Agriculture, forestry & fishing	1.31	1.36	3.58	3.77
2. Mining & quarrying	1.12	1.44	1.52	1.79
3. Manufacturing	1.57	1.85	3.32	2.85
5. Electricity, gas & water	1.37	1.25	2.35	2.30
6. Construction	1.50	1.44	3.19	2.62
7. Trade	1.52	1.77	2.63	2.83
8. Transport & storage	1.32	1.25	2.53	2.03
9. Finance, insurance, real estate & business service	1.50	1.67	2.86	4.12
10.Community, social & personal services	1.40	1.41	3.22	3.38

Source: Shariff and Gumber (1999)

How far trade liberalization has attributed to such employment changes in South Asia is, however, a debated issue. More importantly, most of the employment generation in this region, has been in the unorganized sector that offers little job security for the unskilled workers apart from paying very low and often subsistence wages. Trade liberalization also is changing the composition of employment in favour of the educated and skilled workers contributing to rising wage inequality. For example, in India, rapid trade liberalization reduced average tariff rate from 125 percent to 50 percent between 1990 and 1994. The textile industry was one of the sectors most immediately affected. As the recent Oxfam report (2002) observes, during 1992-1994, in Ahmedabad alone 52 mills closed down with a loss of over 100,000 jobs. Most retrenched workers moved into the informal sectors where reported average wage had been around one-third of what they used to get in the textile industry. On the other hand, trade liberalization has caused a phenomenal growth in exports of information and communication technologies that created some 180,000 jobs during the 1990s. One might put these cases together and say that growth in this sector has overcompensated the losses in the textile sector. But underneath this statistics lies the fact that it is the educated workers who have gained in the process at the cost of less skilled poor workers. Thus employment implications of the restructuring of industries and the changes in production pattern brought about by trade liberalization can be quite complicated than the aggregate employment figures in Table 2.7 might indicate.

Table 2.7

Growth of Labour and Employment in South Asia

	Growth Rate of Labour		Growth Rate of Employment	
	1981 – 85	1986 – 93	1981 – 85	1986 – 93
India	2.02	1.92	1.77	2.37
Pakistan	3.24	2.66	2.07	1.93
Sri Lanka	1.64	1.51	-4.84	12.08

Source: Dev (2000).

2.2 The Wage-Gap Debate: Trade or Technology?

What emerges from the available empirical evidences is that except for a few East Asian countries, there has been widespread and consistent deterioration in relative income position for the unskilled workers. A persistent rise of the ratio of skilled to unskilled wages in US, UK, Latin-America and large parts of Asia indicate such deterioration. Similar increases in wage inequality during 1980s and 1990s have been observed for Australia, Canada, Japan and Sweden [Freeman and Katz (1994), Katz and Autor (1999)]. In Europe, with institutionally fixed unskilled money wages, this has been captured by the loss of employment.

At the theoretical level, economists have been more and more divided on underlying cause(s) of such widespread wage inequality. The debate that has made the general equilibrium trade theory more relevant than ever before [Krugman (2000)], has centered around the relative importance of trade and technology and applicability of standard trade models. Skepticism regarding the trade explanation of the wage inequality stems from the observation that imports of the OECD countries from low-wage countries appear to be too small to account for large variations in wages. The theoretical underpinning of this skepticism and most of the empirical investigations attempting to isolate effects of trade and technology has been the factor content approach that links volume of trade with factor prices *directly*. Several trade theorists tend to reject this view since the factor content approach has very limited applications and anyone familiar with more general trade theory would recognize that volume of trade has no direct impact on the factor prices [Leamer (1998, 2000)].

However, to understand the breadth and depth of this debate it is important to understand the wage determination process in a trading economy. This has been neatly summarized by Jones and Engerman (1996). In the following we describe such a process in the context of a multi-sector and multi-factor open economy.

2.2.1 Wage Determination in General Equilibrium Models

In any general equilibrium (GE) model factor prices are influenced by commodity prices, factor endowments and technology. If P_i, E_i and T_i denote effects of changes in commodity prices, in endowment or factor supply base and in technology respectively then the relative change in price of factor-i is given as,

$$\hat{W}_i = P_i + E_i + T_i \tag{2.1}$$

where, $\hat{W}_i$ represents proportional change in the price of factor-*i*.

The important point to understand in this context is that any other factors, such as trade deficit or surplus, volumes of trade and the like, cannot affect factor prices independent of P_i, E_i and T_i [2].

The effect of these three terms in (2.1) on wages, however, depend on the number of goods versus the number of factors. An economy consuming *m* goods and having *n* factors of production, will produce only *n* goods or less, when *m* > *n*, at a given set of world commodity prices. The *(m - n)* remaining goods will be imported entirely. The even case, number of goods being equal to the number of factors, describe the HOS scenario whereas *m* < *n* describes the specific-factor model a la Jones (1971). In both the even and the *m* > *n* cases, the unique result is that E_i = 0. That is, at given commodity prices, factor prices are uniquely determined. The mechanism through which such a unique relationship holds is simple. In the *m* ≥ *n* case, the competitive price-cost equations or zero-profit conditions for the *m* number of goods produced by the economy are sufficient to determine the prices of the *n* number of factors of production once the commodity

---

[2] Another factor that has no direct influence is the devaluation or revaluation of the nominal exchange rates. Exchange rate changes proportionately raises all commodity prices and money wages leaving relative wages unchanged. Thus, as correctly pointed out by Robbins (1995a), the work on trade and wages by Murphy and Welch (1991) that emphasized the revaluation of the US dollar was based on a false premise.

prices are given from outside[3]. Therefore, given the commodity prices, any change in factor supply or endowment base of the country is accommodated through changes only in the composition of outputs. No changes in factor prices and consequently in factor intensities are needed to clear the domestic factor markets. This often misunderstood one-to-one correspondence between commodity prices and factor prices, given the state of the technology, holds the center-stage of the HOS model and the wage-gap debate. In particular, with P_i being the weighted average of all commodity price changes in absence of any no money illusion, (2.1) boils down to (given the state of technology),

$$\hat{W}_i = \sum_j \beta^i_j \hat{p}_j \qquad (\sum_j \beta^i_j = 1) \qquad (2.2)$$

If θ_{ij} denotes the cost share of factor-i in unit production cost of good-j and $|\theta|$ denotes the determinant of the $n \times n$ cost-share matrix, the weight β^i_j equals the ratio of co-factor of θ_{ij} to $|\theta|$.

Therefore, given the technology, for a trading economy the wages are uniquely determined from outside, no matter how small or large is the volume of trade[4]. Recently, Leamer (1995) has put it in a different way: Even though trade dependence, volume of trade as a proportion of GDP, is low in the US, the existence of a local apparel industry makes the wage of the unskilled workers in the US determined in Shanghai.

Does the unique relationship in (2.2) mean that any increase in the ratio of skilled and unskilled workers in the economy over time through education and training, for example, has no impact on the wage-gap ? The answer depends on the importance of the economy in the world market. With full sectoral factor mobility, such changes in factor endowment must affect the world commodity prices in order to influence the wages. If the country is too small to affect the commodity prices, there would certainly be no changes in wages. Otherwise, with the output composition changing, the world relative price of the skill-intensive commodity will fall through consequent excess supply. Accordingly, given (2.2), the relative wages change. Thus in the $m \geq n$ case, changes in factor endowments can cause factor prices to change only indirectly through changes in commodity prices, if at all. But changes in factor supplies will have a direct influence on factor returns when the number of factors is greater than the number of goods $(m < n)$. Thus, in a specific-factor model, $E \neq 0$.

---

[3] Of course, the production functions for these goods must be different so that the n number of zero-profit conditions constitutes a system of independent equations, and all the factors of production must be sectorally mobile and homogeneous to earn the same wage rate everywhere.
[4] Such one-to-one correspondence holds for all factor prices compatible with full employment even when production technologies exhibit factor intensity reversals.

2.2.2 Industrial Country Experiences: Trade or Technology?

In an early work on trade and wages, labour economists Murphy and Welch (1991) found the evolving pattern of international trade as a "primary cause of recent wage changes" in the US economy. Reich (1991) put it more strongly : Global competition has bifurcated American workers into two groups, the high-earning "symbolic analysts" whose talents are rewarded by globalization and the mass of ordinary production workers whose earnings are dispersed by it. Major incidents in the global economic scene such as the creation of NAFTA, the conclusion of the GATT negotiations, the drive towards the removal of trade barriers, and the growth of imports from the East Asian countries are cited by this group of economists as the primary sources of such widening wage-gap phenomenon.

Despite some evidence, the majority view according to Krugman (2000) is that trade explains only an insignificant part of the US experience. Such skepticism regarding the limited role of trade has arisen from two facts. First are the major technological changes that have occurred in the industrialized countries particularly in US during the last two decades of the twentieth century. Second is the observation that imports of the OECD countries from low-wage countries appear to be too low.

As pointed out by Lawrence (1994), 70 percent of America's manufacturing imports in 1990 came from OECD countries that had similar wage levels. Imports from developing countries amounted to only 2.1 percent of America's GNP. Indeed compared to the 1981 level --- 1.2 percent of GNP --- there had been significant increase in such imports, yet Lawrence remains unpursuaded that such a small change in imports as a percentage of GNP can have a large impact on the overall labour market. On the other hand, Borjas et.al. (1992) concluded that trade flows explained at most 15 percent of the 12.4 percent increase in the earnings differential between college-educated and high-school-educated workers during 1980-88[5]. Similar were the views of Bound and Johnson (1992), Krugman (1995) and Lawrence and Slaughter (1993), that trade volumes are too small to explain large variations in wages in the US.

But from the discussions in the preceding sections it should be immediate that volume of trade or its change matters only when commodity prices are affected. In particular, as long as prices are determined in world markets, changes in commodity prices drive changes in factor prices regardless of trade shares. This

---

[5] Bhagwati and Dahejia (1998) challenges underlying logic of this work by pointing out that Borjas et. al. miss the central point that international trade must affect commodity prices in the desired direction before anything can be inferred about the trade-wage gap nexus. We shall return to this later.

has been strongly reiterated by Leamer (2000, p.20): What matters are whether or not apparel is produced in the US, competing with products made in China.

Despite such strong and unique relationship between commodity and factor prices, why have some economists emphasized so much on the volume of trade? This has been due to a small but interesting piece of empirical methodology, known as factor content approach or *but-for* question, that had originally been used to testing the HO theory [Leamer (1980), Deardorff (1984), Deardorff and Hakura (1994)]. The theoretical basis of this approach as a test for the HO theory had been well laid out in Vanek (1968). Subsequently, it is used by Deardorff and Staiger (1988), Borjas, et. al. (1992), Katz and Murphy (1992) and Wood (1994) to measure the trade (volume) impact on the wage inequality. The basis of such a link is the interpretation of the factor content as a measure of trade-induced changes in factor supplies, and the mis-conception that changes in the factor market necessarily has a direct influence on factor prices in an open economy.

The idea behind this factor content approach is that commodity trade is an implicit kind of factor mobility, which of course is not a new invention but is in fact the essence of the age-old Factor Price Equalization theorem, with the effect of trade on factor prices determined by the net trade embodied in factor services. Suppose we add up the estimate of factors of production that are used in production of exports and from this is subtracted an estimate of inputs that would have been used had imports been domestically produced. The difference represents the factor content of trade or the net exports of factor services embodied in commodity trade, and consequently captures *changes* in effective factor supplies. Alternatively, since trade volume equals excess production, factor content of trade is the difference between the factor quantities used to produce the output vector (X) and those required to produce the consumption vector (C). Algebraically, in the symmetric case ($m = n$), if F denotes an $n \times 1$ vector of net exports of factor services embodied in commodity trade, A denotes the $n \times n$ matrix of input coefficients, a_{ij}, and T denotes the $n \times 1$ vector of trade volumes (or net exports, X - C),

$$F = A(X - C) = AT \qquad (2.3)$$

So AT measures the factor content of trade. When this is subtracted from the vector of actual endowment, V, the difference, V - F, constitutes effective factor supplies. Changes in trade volume produce changes in the factor content and hence can be treated as if they were changes in actual resources. This in turn, as is understood, incorrectly though, triggers changes in factor prices.

In the 2x2 case, with skilled and unskilled labour as the two factors of production, F defined in (2.3) measures *changes* in effective supplies of skilled and unskilled workers. Borjas et. al. (1992) and others then divide the percentage change in the ratio of effective supplies of skilled to unskilled labour by an estimate of the elasticity of substitution to arrive at the estimate of the impact of trade (volume) on relative wages. By this method, if labour services embodied in commodity trade is small, trade cannot have much effect on wages. This is the basis of the argument that US imports from the developing countries are too small to have a large impact on its domestic labour market.

This has raised a considerable amount of controversy among the economists. Trade theorists have almost universally rejected this as an appropriate method of analyzing the trade impact [Bhagwati (1991), Bhagwati and Dahejia (1998), Leamer (1995, 2000) and Panagariya (2000)]. For example, Panagariya (2000) is critical about the restrictive assumptions such as identical elasticity of substitution across all production functions and utility functions that are needed for this approach to measure the contribution of trade to changes in wage inequality with tastes and technology allowed to change. Deardorff (2000) himself has remained cautious in applicability of this approach in the context of wage inequality and has talked about a series of thought experiments where it can and cannot provide us answers we are asking for.

There is a more fundamental issue, which we, like many other trade theorists, reiterate with Leamer (2000): "the connection between factor-content and factor prices is model specific". As discussed in the preceding section, factor supplies can influence factor prices in an open economy, directly *only* in the $m < n$ case, and *only indirectly* through corresponding changes in the world commodity prices (provided, of course, the economy is large enough) in the $m \geq n$ case. Referring back to eq. (2.2), in the $m \geq n$ case, factor prices are completely delinked from factor supplies and, given the state of technology, determined solely by commodity prices that are exogenously given from outside. Thus, changes in trade volumes (or in values) and in the factor-content thereof, have absolutely *no* effect on wages. Such changes are relevant only to the extent that they might affect the commodity prices in the world market. But once again, it is not important to now how large the change is in the trade volume, but how large the change is in commodity prices that such a change in trade volume brings about. Thus the claim that US imports from low-wage countries is too small to cause the observed large changes in wages in the US, requires further empirical investigation beyond the factor content approach to qualify for a well-grounded conclusion.

Changes in goods prices in the world markets are brought about by many factors including trade and technology. Unless we can isolate the extent of price changes that are caused by trade per se, it would not be possible to infer how far the factor price changes induced by changes in goods prices are attributable to trade openness. Krugman (2000) provides a simple example to illustrate the situation. Consider Figure 2.1 where the production possibility curve for the North is drawn. Let P and C be the production and consumption points respectively. It exports a skill-intensive good X to the South and imports an unskilled labour-intensive good Y. What effect has trade on prices? Krugman points out that this is the same as asking what would the relative prices in the North be *but for* the possibility of trading with the South? That is, how much higher would the relative price of good Y be at the autarky point A is the question that is to be addressed.

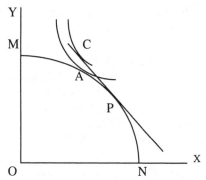

Figure 2.1: The "but-for" Question

He argues that factor content approach essentially addresses the but-for question once it is reinterpreted carefully, and accordingly can be used to isolate the effect of trade from that of technology on commodity prices. But the problem with this is that there might be situations where globalization causes wages to change even at the same level of factor content. The limitation of the factor content approach in isolating the impact of trade from that of technology is best exemplified by Leamer (2000). Consider Figure 2.2 that portrays the domestic labour market in North with a negatively sloped labour demand schedule and a perfectly inelastic labour supply schedule. Suppose the country is small in the usual sense. Consider a Southern country which has perfectly elastic labour supply at the wage W_S. This reflects its competitiveness in the labour-intensive products. Under free trade, the North imports these goods from the South and if factor prices equalize in the two countries, the Northern wage drops to W_S. The corresponding excess demand for labour (that would have arisen if imports were produced in the North) is the factor content of imports from the South. Consider now two changes. One is a technical progress in the North that lowers the demand for labour there, and the other is a fall in the Southern wage rate (may be due to an increase in labour productivity) and consequently in the Northern wage rate. To take an extreme example, suppose these changes are such that the factor content is unaltered. In Figure 2.2 the demand and supply curves are shifted accordingly to keep the excess demand for labour, the factor content of trade, constant.

Does it mean that globalization is unimportant? Certainly not. On the contrary, the fall in wage in the North is entirely due to the globalization effect. Thus as Leamer puts it, "but for the decline in the external value of labour, there would have been no decline in wages and regardless of what was happening to internal supply and demand, exactly the same fall in wages would have occurred". Of course, this exercise is built upon the small country assumption (i.e., upon fixed prices), nevertheless it does point out the kind of problem one might face in isolating the impact of trade from that of technology in this approach.

An alternative way of seeking answer to the but-for question is to calibrate a computable general equilibrium (CGE) model to the actual data, including the volume of trade, and to calculate the difference between the actual relative price and the relative price consistent with autarky. The implied difference between actual and autarky factor prices thus may be regarded as the effect of trade on factor prices. Applying this method, Krugman (1995) has found that the North-South trade has lowered the relative price of unskilled labour-intensive products by less than 1 percent, and the relative wage of unskilled workers by less than 3 percent. That is, trade has caused a "significant but fairly small fraction of massive increase in wage inequality in advanced countries".

Of late, Feenstra and Hanson (2001) argue that the ratio of trade to GDP for the industrial economies does not tell us the whole story. Since services rather than merchandise such as manufacturing, mining and agriculture, have increasing shares of GDP in almost all these countries, to make a better evaluation of the role of trade there, one should compare (merchandise) trade to merchandise value added. On such comparisons, except for countries like Australia, Japan and UK, all other industrial countries have experienced substantial growth in trade in 1990 compared to what they had in 1913. Thus, it may be incorrect to say that trade has not had any significant role in the increasing wage inequality or employment changes. They demonstrate that outsourcing or trade in fragments can explain such links. Such trade has much the same impact on labour demand as does the skill-biased technological progress.

Bernard and Jensen (1997) also provide some evidence that trade has had some impact on factor demand and wages. Increased trade usually changes the relative

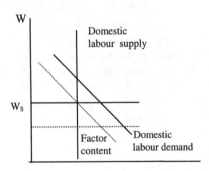

Figure 2.2: Labour Content of Trade

employment of skilled workers across the industries whereas new technology shifts such employment within industries. Given such effects, skepticism regarding the dominant role of trade has been rooted in the observation of Berman et. al. (1994) that within industry movements had been larger than across industry movements in many industrial countries. But replacing their industry-level data by plant-level data, Bernard and Jensen found significant movements across the manufacturing plants.

Thus, whether growing wage inequality had been brought about by freer trade or new technology is essentially an empirical rather than a theoretical question.

2.2.3 If Technology, Sector or Factor Bias?

The other facet of the theoretical debate is the sector versus factor bias of the technological change. In a standard general equilibrium model, such as the one described earlier, factor-bias technical progress does not really matter. As explained by Jones and Engerman (1996), effect of a technological change on wages can be decomposed as,

$$T = \sum_j \beta_j \pi_j \qquad (2.4)$$

where π_j is a Hicksian measure of the degree of technical progress in industry j. This is defined as the relative reduction in unit costs at constant factor prices. No role of any factor bias is indicated by (2.4). It seems all that matters is sector-bias. If technical progress takes place in skill-intensive sector, the wage-gap must widen regardless of the factor-bias of such technical progress.

This caveat is just the mirror image of the irrelevance of factor endowments or supplies. However, two important conditions must hold. One is that commodity prices are constant and that is possible only when the country is small, and the other is that the technical progress is unilateral. Of late, Krugman (2000) argues that both these are wrong thought experiments in the current state of controversies. Once we recognize that technical progress has taken place in a large country like US and also simultaneously in few other OECD countries that can at least collectively affect world commodity prices, it is easy to understand that skill-bias of such technical progress that has been observed is at the root of the wage-gap phenomenon.

2.2.4 The Developing Countries: Role of Trade

While there may be some germs of truth in arguments attributing wage inequality in large advanced countries to technical change, the case is not so strong for the developing countries. First of all, it should be kept in mind that in the past few decades not much significant technological improvement has taken place in the developing world that could affect world prices and consequently wage inequality. On the other hand, unilateral technological change in North can affect wage inequality in South only through trade between these countries. By the but-for approach, with no trade taking place and consequently Southern prices delinked from world markets, Southern wages are determined solely by internal factors. Thus, (unilateral) technical progress in the North cannot in any way affect wages in the South. Of course, one might put revolution in information technology (IT) in a developing country like India that has positively affected wages of the IT experts there as a point in case for technology-led changes in the wage inequality. But such technological changes are in large part brought about by the trade opportunities and consequent increased demand for peripherals. In particular, we believe that increasing returns to human capital in the developing countries is still linked with trade.

Such trade or trade-induced-technological-change stories can also be traced down to whatever little evidence regarding wage inequality in South is available. The empirically observed strong association between trade liberalization and widening wage-gap in Latin America is shown in Table 2.8. Except in cases of second-phase liberalization programmes in Argentina and in Chile, the wage-gap widened with reduction of trade barriers. In Chile average tariff rates were reduced from over 100 percent prior to 1975 to 11 percent by 1979. Openness rose from about twenty to fifty-five percent during 1970-1990.

Table 2.8

Effects of Increased Openness in Latin-American Countries

Country & Years	Changes in Trade Reform	Wage-Gap	Relative Demand for Skill
Argentina 1977-82	Barrier reduction with appreciation	Widened	Rising
1989-93	Barrier reduction with appreciation	Narrowed	Falling
Chile 1974-79	Barrier reduction with devaluation	Widened	Rising
Colombia 1985-94	Barrier reduction during 1990-92	Widened	Rising
Costa Rica 1985-93	Barrier reduction and devaluation	Widened (1988-90)	Rising
Uruguay 1990-95	Barrier reduction	Widened	Rising

Source: As reported in Wood (1997).

Though during 1976-1989 Colombia did not liberalize its trade regime significantly, its currency was devalued over 60 percent between 1985 and 1989. The openness there hovered roughly around twenty-five percent.

In almost all these cases the relative demand for skill workers has been found to be rising pointing towards a possible trade-wage-gap nexus. Beyer et. al. (1999) find that wage inequality in Chile in last two decades of the twentieth century is more due to trade-induced changes in production structure of the economy than technology transfer or skill-biased technical progress. At the same time there is clear indication in their study that increasing the relative supply of college graduates reduces wage inequality. Mexico is another example where skilled-unskilled wage-gap increased in parallel with radical trade liberalization. The survey by the Mexican Ministry of Trade identified nonproduction workers as skilled and production workers as unskilled. It was found that between 1984 and 1990 the ratio of average hourly wages of nonproduction and production workers increased from 1.93 to 2.55 (see Table 2.9). During that period, tariffs were reduced there by 45 percents and import licenses by more than 75 percent.

Table 2.9

Tariff and Wage Inequality in Mexico
in Manufacturing Sector at 1980 Prices

Year	Ratio of hourly wages of non-production and production workers	Average Tariff
1984	1.930	-
1985	1.948	25.2
1986	2.027	22.6
1987	2.018	11.8
1988	2.166	11.3
1989	2.398	13.1
1990	2.545	-

Source: Feenstra and Hanson (1996); WTO.

At the same time, in Mexico the increasing wage-gap during 1984-1990 coincided with the steep decline in the real minimum wage. Similarly, in Chile following the military overthrow of the Alende government in late 1970s, union power was contained and wage differentials were restored to the levels prevailing in the 1960s. The curtailment of union power as another explanation of the wage-gap hypothesis is, therefore, hard to rule out [Wood (1997)]. However, such explanations which may hold partly for Mexico and Chile, as we will show later in Chapter 9, cannot be used to explain the experiences of India, Colombia, Costa Rica and Uruguay.

The trade story seems to be appropriate for a few Asian countries also. For example, for Sri Lanka, the period 1977-1985 during which widening of wage-gap has been observed (Table 2.5) had witnessed some radical changes in economic policy in favour of a more open economy. The average tariff during 1983-85 was reduced by 25 percent. The Indian experience reported in Table 2.6 also indicates that the trade openness might have some telling impact on growing wage inequality as the phenomenon coincides with its period of drastic trade and exchange rate reforms. Substantial devaluation of the domestic currency with relaxing of exchange control and partial convertibility of the foreign currency was undertaken in 1991-1993. The average tariff rate was reduced drastically from 79.2 in 1991 to 47.8 in 1993. All these contributed to an increase in the openness index from an average level of 2.8 percent in 1986-89 to 4.2 percent by 1995. Growing inequality in China and Hong Kong seem to be driven at least partly by opening up of markets to foreign trade and investment.

Of late Mohan Rao (1999) has examined impact of trade openness on income inequality in the developing countries. The intriguing feature of his analysis is the construction of a trade index as opposed to the standard trade ratio or export to GDP ratio index accommodating for the size and per capita income of the trading countries. He finds a positive and statistically significant relationship between changes in the trade index measure of openness and changes in poverty in the developing countries. There is also a positive though statistically insignificant relationship between trend in inequality and that in openness. Not surprisingly, however, poverty and income inequality are positively correlated.

Our own preliminary observation in this regard, reported in Table 2.10, reveals asymmetric effect of trade liberalization on income inequality over time for some of the developing countries. We consider both the Gini coefficient and the share of income of the top decile group relative to that of the bottom decile group of population   (D10/D1) for the period 1991-98. For countries like Brazil, El Salvador, Honduras, India and Philippines, both these measures of income inequality appear to be inversely related with their respective average tariff rates during 1994-95 and 1997-98. But for Bulgaria, Estonia, Latvia and Paraguay, tariff changes have significantly different effects on these two measures. Whereas the Gini coefficient has increased (or decreased) with the reduction (or increase) in the average tariff rates, the relative income shares have moved in exactly the opposite way for these countries.

The cross-country relationship between average tariff and relative income shares for 1997-98, on the other hand, does indicate the adverse effect of trade liberalization (Figure 2.3). Similar inverse relationship has been found for these countries in 1994-95. Though a more detail investigation to such causation is required before we can argue more convincingly, these observations are quite in line with the findings of Mohan Rao (1999).

Table 2.10

Tariff and Income Inequality in Developing Countries: 1991-1998

Country	1991-92/1994-95			1997-98		
	Avg. Tariff	Gini	D10/D1	Avg. Tariff	Gini	D10/D1
Brazil	11.10	60.10	59.88	11.80	59.10	46.70
Bulgaria (1991-2)	17.90	24.23	7.48	16.60	26.40	5.07
China	25.00	41.50	14.05	16.80	40.30	12.67
El Salvador	10.20	49.90	31.90	8.00	50.80	28.07
Estonia	5.50	36.63	11.91	0.00	37.60	9.93
Ghana (1991-92)	17.00	33.91		8.50	39.60	12.29
Honduras	9.70	53.70	35.08	8.50	59.00	110.75
India	41.00	29.70	6.10	35.00	37.80	9.57
Latvia	5.00	28.50	6.78	5.90	32.40	8.93
Pakistan (1991-2)	61.10	31.15		41.70	31.20	6.73
Paraguay	9.30	59.10	66.5	11.20	57.70	87.60
Peru	15.00	44.87	22.13	13.30	46.50	22.12
Philippines	20.00	42.90	13.96	13.40	46.20	15.91
Thailand (1991-2)	38.00	51.50	14.84	20.10	41.40	11.57
Venezuela	13.40	46.80	23.73	11.90	48.80	23.50
Zambia (1991-92)	26.00	43.51		6.80	52.60	37.27

Source: Compiled from Deininger and Squire (1997) data set, World Development Report and WTO.

On the other hand, as evident from Table 2.11, the empirical evidence regarding the disemployment effect of trade liberalization is mixed. Unemployment increased in Chile, Colombia, Philippines (first phase), Spain, Turkey and Yugoslavia during their respective liberalization periods. In Israel the deferred liberalization programmes significantly reduced unemployment. For Philippines in the second phase, and for Argentina, Korea and Peru, on the other hand, unemployment decreased. The Indian experience is bit ambiguous. The rising unemployment during 1991-1994 during its period of exchange rate liberalization observed by Dutt (1994) is in contradiction with the increase in growth rate of employment above the growth rate of the workforce recorded by Dev (2000) as mentioned earlier.

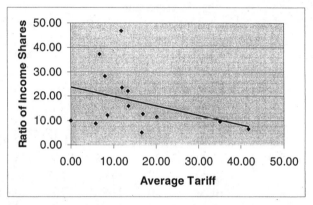

Figure 2.3: Trade Liberalization and Income Distribution
in Selected Developing Countries (1997-98)

Wood and Calandrino (2001) have evaluated the effect of increased trade on the employment structures in India and China. Their calculations are based on construction of the Social Accounting Matrices for 1994-95 in case of India and for 1997 for China. Their estimate reveals that 5 percent of total employment in the skill-intensive manufacturing sectors in India is generated by exports. On the other hand, foreign trade or *net* exports account for 11.4 and 7.1 percents of employment in the unskilled labour-intensive manufacture in India and China respectively. Moreover, they observe that whereas trade reduces employment of illiterates by 3 percent in India, employment of the college graduates rises by half a percent.

2.3 Issues: What Do We Need to Address ?

Part of the misperception about the trade explanation is due to the mindset of trade theorists in applying HOS model and its minor variants to capture the effect of trade on wage inequality. These models are too simple to capture the complex relationship between trade and factor prices. Analytical convenience has often been given preference over reality. Instead of building up models that are better approximations of dual production structures, labour market characteristics and peculiarities of the developing countries, economists have reduced the debate to one of trade versus technology. These two issues should be addressed separately. Moreover, one might argue how far the factor content approach that is couched in terms of the HOS model can be of use because of the inappropriateness of the HOS structure itself as a model of the developing countries.

Table 2.11
Liberalization and Unemployment in Selected Countries During 1965-85

Country	Reform Period	Unemployment (percent of labour force)		
		a	b	c
Argentina	1967 - 70	5.6	5.1	4.9
Chile	1974 - 81	4.8	12.3	12.4
Colombia	1964 - 66	7.9	8.7	10.1
	1968 - 82	8.8	10.0	9.4
Israel	1969 - 77	6.1	3.4	3.9
Korea	1965 - 67	9.9	7.0	6.3
	1978 - 79	4.1	3.5	3.8
Peru	1979 - 80	7.1	6.9	6.8
Philippines	1960 - 65	6.3	8.0	8.2
	1970 - 74	6.9	6.5	4.7
Spain	1977 - 80	5.3	9.1	11.5
Turkey	1980 - 84	9.4	11.7	12.7
Yugoslavia	1965 - 67	5.6	6.6	7.1
India	1991 - 94	3.1	4.6	5.5

Notes : a. Average of three years prior to the year of liberalization
b. Year of liberalization
c. Average of three years after the year of liberalization
Source : Michaely, et. al., 1991; World Development Indicators.

Given the empirical evidence, any explanation and the underlying model must be able to generate symmetric changes in wage inequality across nations. Since opening up or liberalization of trade asymmetrically affect goods prices faced by the trading nations, the implied factor price changes is expected to be asymmetric as well going by the standard trade theories. But as mentioned earlier, this is largely at variance with the empirical observation. The major task at hand therefore should be recasting the neoclassical relationship between prices of goods and factors. Unfortunately, not much attention has been paid this regard. The discussions of possible impact of trade on wages have so far been centered on the wage inequality in the North or in the South. But what needs to be done is to join these piecemeal analyses to carry out a proper thought experiment that is consistent with the empirical observations. Moreover, while theorists have been pouring in materials to justify the observed pattern of wage movements in the developed world, very little has been said to highlight theoretical consequences of trade on wage inequality in the South. Even if the South is wide and diverse, we do believe that appropriate theoretical constructs can be very useful.

The first step towards this is to build up models that capture the essence of trade and production structures in the South. One such feature is the bimodal comparative advantage and diverse trade pattern involving exports of both skill and unskilled intensive products that many Southern countries are showing up in their basket. India is, of course, our prime example. Once this is recognized, given the wage-price relationship, it is not hard to explain rising wage inequality even if the share of skill-intensive products in total exports of Southern countries is not significant enough.

The second aspect that has far reaching implications for the trade-employment relationship is the segmented labour markets in the developing countries. Quite a sizeable proportion of the unskilled workforce ranging from 60 to 90 percent finds employment in the unorganized or informal sectors. In India, as in other developing countries, agriculture is one typical example where share of unorganized sector is staggering 99 percent. The paradox of low unemployment rates in many developing countries is also to be analyzed from this perspective. The poor are too poor to remain unemployed. Thus they often offer their work for bare subsistence wage or are self-employed managing to earn paltry sum of money resulting in low rates of unemployment but high rates of poverty by any standard. These people are in fact underemployed. Under such circumstances, overall employment figures do not indicate the real position of the unskilled.

The Indian scenario presented in Table 2.12 is a typical example in this regard. In agriculture, manufacturing and construction, employment shares of the unorganized or informal sectors are staggeringly high. The shares of unorganized sector in mining & quarrying and transport & storage have also increased substantially. These figures are enough to indicate that overall employment growth in India may have been accompanied by reallocation of workforce towards the low-wage unorganized or informal sectors.

Is this sufficient to infer that trade-reform is harmful? Not necessarily. Expansion of the informal sector may imply lower or higher informal wage. Since both demand and supply play their part in determining the size of this sector, employment figures only do not allow us to infer anything. As we argue later by drawing from Marjit (2000), if downsizing formal sector means flight of capital into the informal sector, then such a process is welcome. Otherwise not. Hence, the important empirical investigation should be whether the share of capital allocated to the informal sector has also increased in the process. This theoretical understanding is absolutely essential if one has to draw any inference from the growing size of the informal segment. Any serious attempt to address the trade-employment or trade-wages relationship must, therefore, deal with these aspects of covered and uncovered labour markets. Changing distribution of employment across these markets, and changing pattern of disguised unemployment and/or underemployment in the unorganized sectors should be at the centre-stage of analysis, instead of the impact of trade on wages and aggregate employment. This is what part of this book aims at.

Table 2.12
Share of Unorganized Sector Employment in India

Sector	1988	1994
Agriculture	99.3	99.4
Mining & quarrying	54.7	59.0
Manufacturing	81.1	82.1
Electricity, gas & water	0	0
Construction	90.0	89.1
Transport, storage	62.8	71.1
Total Organized	90.1	91.1

Source: ILO (1996); Annual & Quarterly Employment Review, Ministry of Labour, New Delhi.

The trade-induced changes in the production of the non-traded good is the other potential source of growing wage inequality in the South since most of the non-traded production in the LDCs use unskilled labour intensively. The more important issue, however, is whether non-traded production is organized in the informal or in the formal sector. Essentially the way formal and informal sectors are modeled in the literature the issue at hand can be rephrased as examining the role of the non-traded production under alternative wage formation assumption: (higher) contractual unskilled wage or fully flexible market-determined unskilled wage. Since the traded sectors compete with the non-traded sectors for the scarce resources they commonly use and the non-traded production by definition must match its domestic demand, trade liberalization induced expansion of activities in the traded sectors will be possible only through a fall in the demand for non-tradable. This necessitates an increase in the price of non-traded goods and consequent changes in the domestic income distribution. Herein comes the role of the nature of the non-traded sector.

Finally one should look into the implications of the skill information process induced by globalization. Deregulation, liberalization or increasing degree of integration with the rest of the world do create expanding opportunities for the talented and skilled people. The contribution of such a process should not be undermined. But the major problem can still be the one which does not allow a significant chunk of the population to avail of these global opportunities. Basic education and financial capabilities to tap on the benefits of the process and expand along with the growth may still not be available to a large number of people and therefore the process may entail a fairly long phase of sustained and possibly growing inequality.

II

EXPLAINING SYMMETRIC WAGE-GAP

3 THE STANDARD TRADE THEORY: HOW FAR DOES IT GO?

3.1 Introduction

The theory underlying the debate on the link between trade liberalization and widening wage-gap has been the Heckscher-Ohlin-Samuelson (HOS) model of trade. The cornerstone of the trade theorists' argument is one of its core propositions, the celebrated Stolper-Samuelson theorem : Increased unskilled labour-intensive imports from countries such as China or Mexico and the consequent fall in the domestic price of the import-competing goods in the US depresses the unskilled wage and raises the skill wage thereby widening the wage-gap. There are, however, two major problems with this argument. First, there is no clear empirical evidence regarding the fall in the domestic price of the unskilled labour-intensive import-competing goods in the US which triggers the Stolper-Samuelson result, i.e., causes the relative wage to move against the unskilled labour [Bhagwati (1995), Leamer (1995)]. Second, following the Heckscher-Ohlin argument, increased trade with the developed countries (DCs) should imply a declining wage-gap in the less developed countries (LDCs) abundant in the unskilled labour. But, as mentioned earlier, this has not happened in Latin America and in large parts of Asia.

The failure to explain the symmetric changes in the wage-gap in the trading nations with asymmetric endowment and trade patterns has raised serious doubts about the straightjacket application of HOS model. On the other hand, findings of Robbins (1996a) of strong domestic supply impact on relative wages suggest forces that are more consistent with some variant of specific-factors model of trade instead of the HOS structure.

In this chapter we review the theoretical background of the trade-related debate and examine how far the HOS and specific-factors models take us to explain the more or less similar changes in the wage-gap in most part of the globe.

3.2 Trade and Income Distribution in the HOS Model

The dominant undercurrent of the neoclassical trade theory is the Heckscher-Ohlin-Samuelson (HOS) model linking a country's comparative advantage to its exogenously given factor endowment base at any point of time. Relative abundance of physical capital in one country compared to another makes it a cheaper source of supply of the relatively capital-intensive commodity and conversely a high-cost producer of the relatively labour-intensive commodities.

Thus, the capital-abundant countries tend to specialize and export relatively capital-intensive commodities and import labour intensive commodities. Of course such a Heckscher-Ohlin (HO) or factor proportions story requires production technology for any good to be the same across all trading nations and identical and homothetic tastes[6]. If technologies differ across the trading nations, it *per se* can explain the pattern of trade and gains to be had from such trade a la David Ricardo[7]. The primary concern of Heckscher and Ohlin was, however, to analyze the direction of trade and its implications for countries that share the identical technology for producing goods. Thus the commodities in the HOS model are in a sense standardized products such as the manufacturing goods.

The homotheticity of tastes, on the other hand, makes the direction of trade independent of the size of the trading nations. But that is not sufficient. If the consumers in the home country have a taste bias compared to their foreign counterparts in the good which uses intensively the relatively abundant factor, the actual pattern of trade between the home and foreign country may be quite opposite to what the HO theory predicts. This taste bias argument is often used to explain Leontief's (1956) findings that though after the World War II the US emerged as the most capital-rich industrial country, its trade pattern was that of a labour-abundant country. Leontief's own position regarding this seemingly paradoxical observation was that since the US workers were more productive than their counterparts elsewhere, essentially the US was relatively abundant in (effective) labour. His position has recently been reaffirmed by Trefler (1993).

Figure 3.1 illustrates the case in the standard 2x2x2 case. The upward sloping curve labeled s_1 depicts the relationship between relative supply and relative price of labour-intensive good X in the labour-rich home country[8]. This curve lies below the curve s_1^* depicting similar relationship in the foreign country. This essentially reflects the labour-rich home country's production bias in the labour-intensive good X and conversely foreign country's production bias in capital-intensive good[9]. With homothetic and identical taste in the two countries represented by the same relative demand curve d_1, these production biases get translated into a

---

[6] Absence of any factor intensity reversals is another condition underlying this pattern of trade.

[7] For a textbook exposition of Ricardian trade see Caves, Frankel and Jones (1997).

[8] We adopt the physical definition of factor-abundance by which the home (foreign) country is relatively labour (capital) rich if and only if $K/L < K^*/L^*$, where variables with asterisk apply to the foreign country. This should be distinguished from the *price definition* that identifies home country as labour-rich when the wage-rental ratio in the home country is smaller than that in the foreign country.

[9] An alternative interpretation of s_1 lying to the right of s_1^* reflects what is known as the Rybczynski Theorem: If labour force grows faster than accumulation of physical capital, for any given set of commodity prices the production of good X increases faster than the growth in labour force and the increase in production of good Y, if at all, lags behind the accumulation of capital (implying thereby an increase in relative supply

comparative advantage of home country in good X and of foreign country in good Y as revealed by the autarkic (relative) price comparisons : $p_a < p_a^*$. The labour-rich home country, therefore, exports labour-intensive good X and imports capital-intensive good Y which is the HO theorem.

But if the foreign consumers have taste bias in the capital intensive good Y, the relative demand curve for the country, d_1^*, lies to the left of d_1. In such a situation we may well end up with point B as the autarkic equilibrium in the foreign country in which case the actual trade pattern would be reverse of what the HO theory predicts[10]: Labour-rich home country exporting capital-intensive good Y and importing labour-intensive good X from capital-rich foreign country. The reason is simple. The labour-rich home country's production bias makes it a larger producer of good X compared to the foreign country. But if the (relative) demand for good X is high enough in the home country than in the foreign country due to taste bias of the home consumers, the implied scarcity of good X raises its (relative) price at home above that in the foreign country.

This role of demand in fact demonstrates how the comparative advantage may differ from the doctrine of comparative cost advantage as expounded separately by Torrens and Ricardo. With the comparative advantage, described by the differences in the autarchic relative prices across the trading nations, dictating trade and its direction, the comparative cost advantage arising out of superior technology or factor endowment bias may not be consistent with the observed pattern of trade.

Along with the issue of direction of trade between countries having asymmetric factor endowments, the trade-income distribution relationship has been the major concern of the HOS model. Two important results focus on such relationship:

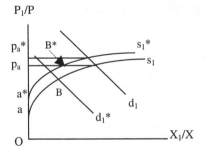

Figure 3.1: HOS Trade Pattern

---

[10] At worst there may not even be any trade taking place when the trade bias and production bias are equal in magnitude. In terms of Figure 3.1, this happens to be the case when d_1^* intersects s_1^* at B*.

Factor Price Equalization (FPE) Theorem: Free commodity trade between countries equalizes the rate of return to the factors in the two countries [Samuelson (1948)]. That is, commodity trade acts as substitute of factor trade.

Stolper-Samuelson (SS) Theorem: Free commodity trade unambiguously raises the real return to the abundant factor and reduces the real return to the scarce factor [Stolper and Samuelson (1941)][11].

Whereas the FPE Theorem is the essence of the one-to-one correspondence between prices of traded goods and (non-traded) factors of production in an open economy, the much-celebrated SS Theorem is directly relevant for what we pursue in this book.

The SS Theorem in its restricted form as stated above, depends crucially on the validity of the HO theorem itself. But if for reasons spelled out the labour-rich country exports the relatively capital-intensive good, trade liberalization implies an increase in the real return to the scarce factor, capital, rather than that of the abundant factor, labour. We, therefore, focus on a more generalized statement that is independent of the abundance or scarcity of factors and hence of the validity of the HOS theorem, known as the *price magnification effect* [Jones (1965, 1979)]. It states that free trade raises the real return to the factor used intensively in production of exportables and conversely reduces the real return to the factor used intensively in production of importables.

To fix ideas and relate this price magnification effect to the phenomenon of widening wage-gap, consider a home country producing exportables good X and importables good Y using skilled labour, S, and unskilled labour, L. With all markets perfectly competitive, competitive forces drive down profits to zero in each sector. Thus, commodity market equilibrium (under autarky) is described by following equalities of price and average cost :

$$P_X = a_{SX}W_S + a_{LX}W \tag{3.1}$$

$$P_Y = a_{SY}W_S + a_{LY}W \tag{3.2}$$

where W_S and W are money wages to skilled and unskilled workers respectively and a_{ij}, denotes per unit requirement of the i-th factor in j-th production that are decided on the basis cost minimization pursuits of the producers :

---

[11] The original statement of the SS theorem was that tariff protection raises the real return to the scarce factor and lowers that of the abundant factor. This compares the free trade situation with restricted trade and, therefore, is different from the statement given above that compares free trade with autarky.

$$a_{ij} = a_{ij}(W_s, W) , \quad i = S, l; j = X, Y \tag{3.3}$$

On the other hand, flexibility of the factor prices ensure that domestic factor markets clear, i.e., both skilled and unskilled workers are fully employed :

$$\overline{S} = a_{SX} X + a_{SY} Y \tag{3.4}$$

$$\overline{L} = a_{LX} X + a_{LY} Y \tag{3.5}$$

where $\overline{S}$ and $\overline{L}$ are given endowments of skilled and unskilled workers and X and Y are the output levels.

Equation system (3.1) - (3.5) describe the supply side of the HOS model. For any given set of commodity prices the factor prices and corresponding input choices are determined by (3.1) - (3.3). Finally, given these input coefficients, the full employment conditions determine the output levels. Any change in the commodity prices affect these outputs through changes in input choices consequent upon the induced factor price changes. The emerging supply relationship is the one shown in Figure 3.1.

An alternative diagrammatic approach to the derivation of such supply relationship would be in terms of the production possibility curve (PPC) shown in Figure 3.2. The PPC is the locus of different combinations of full employment output levels corresponding to different factor prices and consequent input choices. Thus, at any point on the PPC the full employment conditions (3.4) and (3.5) are satisfied. The bowed out shape of the PPC reflects the increasing opportunity cost or the diminishing marginal rate of transformation (MRT) of production of good Y into that of good X.

Now, perfect competition implies that the price of each good be equal to its marginal cost (MC) of production. In this two good case, this amounts to equality between the relative price of good X and the ratio of MCs which in turn is the MRT in absence of any production externality. Therefore, for any given relative price, say p_a, equilibrium relative supply is determined by the tangency between the corresponding price line and the PPC. Let p_{min} denote a very low relative price of X for which the price line is tangent to the PPC at the corner point A. This is the price for which the production of good X is just viable. Thus, for all $p \leq p_{min}$, the country produces only good Y so that the relative supply of good X is zero. Referring back to Figure 1, the vertical intercept Oa equals such a relative price of good X. Similarly, p_{max} is a very low relative price of good Y for which its production ceases altogether. That is, for all $p \geq p_{max}$ the country produces only good X. For any intermediate price, the country is incompletely specialized and tends to produce more of good X and less of good Y as the relative price of good X increases.

Given homothetic taste, such a positively sloped relative supply curve together with the relative demand curve for good X (denoted by d_1 in Figure 3.1) determines the autarkic relative price p_a uniquely.

Consider now a foreign country with similar set up. Let p_a^* be the autarchic equilibrium price in this foreign country. Our assumption that home country exports good X, i.e., it has a comparative advantage in good X, implies,

$$p_a < p_a^* \tag{3.6}$$

Such a comparative advantage may reflect production bias of home country arising out of superior technology in production of X or relative abundance of unskilled labour there, or simply the taste-bias, or both. Whatever may be the source of such comparative advantage or price differences, through arbitrage (buying cheap and selling dear) and consequent physical movements of goods across the national borders, the domestic prices will eventually be equalized across the globe, say at a level $\bar{p}$, thereby stopping any further movements of goods.

How are the factor prices expected to change consequent upon such commodity price movements? Suppose the exportables are relatively unskilled-labour intensive. With the increase in the relative price of exportables, production of the import-competing good-Y contracts and that of good-X increases. The consequent resource reallocation leads to an excess demand for unskilled labour and an excess supply of skilled labour because the expanding X-sector requires more unskilled labour and can absorb fewer skilled labour than are released by the contracting Y-sector. Hence, the unskilled money wage increases whereas the skilled money wage declines. However, we can say something more than just these changes in the absolute prices.

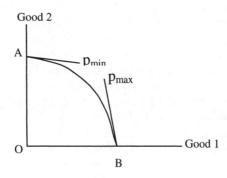

Figure 3.2: PPC in the HOS Model

An appeal to the SS theorem indicates that freer trade causes the real wage to increase and the real return to skilled labour to fall (see appendix)[12] :

$$\hat{W} > \hat{P}_X > 0 > \hat{P}_Y > \hat{W}_S \qquad (3.7)$$

Conversely, in the foreign country similar argument leads to,

$$\hat{W}_S^* > \hat{P}_Y^* > 0 > \hat{P}_X^* > \hat{W}^* \qquad (3.8)$$

That is, free trade makes foreign skilled workers better-off and unskilled workers worse-off.

Note that the factor content of trade, AT, as can be recalled from (2.3), does not play any role in determining the wage movements, either its magnitude or its direction. In this symmetric case ($m = n = 2$), the factor prices are linked to the world commodity prices that are given exogenously. If $\overline{P}_x$ and $\overline{P}_Y$ denote the world prices corresponding to $\overline{p}$, factor prices are determined uniquely by the zero-profit conditions [(3.1) and (3.2) at home, and by similar conditions that hold abroad], regardless of the factor content of trade and corresponding adjustment in the factor markets whatsoever.

What the above price magnification effects or the (generalized) SS theorems indicate is that trade liberalization causes the wage-gap to change *asymmetrically* in the two countries. Since the LDCs or the Southern countries are observed to be exporting predominantly the labour intensive commodities compared to the industrialized nations or the North, we can interpret the home country in our example as the South and the foreign country as the North[13]. On this interpretation, whereas the SS result (3.8) explains the widening wage-gap in the North, (3.7) is at variance with what has been observed in most of the Latin-American and South-East Asian countries as documented earlier. Therefore, the HOS model with the SS theorem at its core does not take us very far in explaining the more or less similar income distributional effects of free trade observed in the North and in the South.

There is one exception, however, of the above asymmetric effect in the standard framework. Suppose production technology exhibits factor intensity reversal (FIR) such that,

---

[12] Throughout this book "hat" over a variable implies proportionate change, e.g., $\hat{P} = dP / P$.

[13] We shall deviate from this interpretation later in a multi-commodity setting that allows us to incorporate the emerging diversified export basket of the South.

$$l_X < l_Y \, \forall \rho \in \left]0, \overline{\rho}\right] \tag{3.9a}$$

$$l_X > l_Y \, \forall \rho \in \left[\overline{\rho}, \infty\right] \tag{3.9b}$$

where $l_j \equiv S_j/L_j$ = skilled-unskilled labour intensity in sector-j and ρ is the unskilled-skill wage ratio.

Thus, the intensity lines in Figure 3.3 cross each other at $\overline{\rho}$. Such factor intensity reversal arises when the production technology is such that the isoquants for good-X and good-Y intersect each other twice or are mutually tangent. Consequently the one-to-one correspondence between commodity and factor prices no longer holds. This is shown by the curve mnm' in the lower panel in Figure 3.3. However, given the factor endowment of the country, the factor prices compatible with full employment are restricted and for these values the commodities can still be ranked uniquely. Consequently, in practice the one-to-one correspondence can be obtained. For example, given home country's endowment line l, cd defines the equilibrium factor price range so that at equilibrium good-X is unequivocally relatively unskilled-labour intensive and mn is the relevant curve capturing the one-to-one correspondence there.

Now, if foreign country's endowments are significantly different as given by the line l^* the ranking of goods in the two countries at respective equilibrium are diametrically opposite leading to symmetric changes in the wage-gaps.

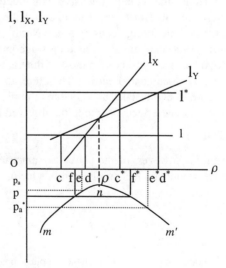

Figure 3.3: Factor Intensity Reversal and
Symmetric Wage Movement

This is because the commodity price changes now affect the factor prices *asymmetrically* in the two countries. Thus with asymmetric commodity price movements through trade, the consequent factor price movements become symmetric. For example, suppose in Figure 3.3, p_a and $p_a{}^*$ are the autarkic relative commodity prices in home and foreign countries with e and e^* as the corresponding autarkic equilibrium factor prices. With trade opening up and home (foreign) country exporting good-X (good-Y), the world commodity price settles at $\bar{p}$. Consequently, unskilled-skilled wage ratio falls in both the countries --- from e to f in home and from e^* to f^* abroad. The wage-gap, therefore, widens in both North and South.

In sum, factor intensity reversal with significant endowment differences across the trading nations can yield symmetric changes in the wage-gap as is empirically observed[14]. However, this is an exception rather than a rule.

3.3 The Specific-Factor Model of Trade and Income Distribution

One important property of the HOS model is the independence of wages from endowments of skilled and unskilled workers. Any changes in such factor supplies can affect wages only through changes in world commodity prices and that too when the country is an important trader in the world market. Recall from our earlier discussion in Chapter 2 that this means, for a small open economy (or as a matter fact, for a given set of world prices), $E = 0$, as long as $m \geq n$. But findings of Robbins (1996a) of strong domestic supply impact on relative wages in Colombia suggest forces inconsistent with this property of the HOS model.

As pointed out earlier, in the specific-factor model of trade where the number of factors of production is greater than the number of traded goods, the endowment base of the economy has a direct influence on wages. It may appear obvious then to presuppose better applicability of such a model on the basis of findings of Robbins (1996a). But the specific-factor model too cannot explain the symmetric changes in the wage-gap in the trading nations. To illustrate this point we consider here the 2-commodity, 3-factor (or the specific-factor) model a la Jones (1971). There are three factors of production: skilled labour, unskilled labour and capital (K). Not all these factors are used in both the production activities. In Jones (1971), with two types of capital being sector-specific in use, only (homogeneous)

---

[14] Note if endowment differences are not significant so that incomplete specialization ranges cd and c^*d^* lie on the same side of $\bar{p}$ in Figure 3.3, commodities are ranked similarly in the two countries. Accordingly, factor price changes following commodity price movements through trade are also similar. In such a case once again we get asymmetric changes --- declining wage-gap in one country and widening wage-gap in the other.

labour was used in both the sectors. In our specification, with two types of labour, it is natural to think of skilled and unskilled workers being specific to the two sectors with (homogeneous) capital being used in producing both the goods[15].

3.3.1 Skilled Labour Specific in Production of Southern Importables

Consider once again two countries labeled as the North and the South (or foreign and home, respectively), producing two goods, X and Y. Good X is a manufacturing good requiring skilled labour along with capital, whereas good Y is an agricultural good that requires no (or only basic) skill along with capital. To keep the spirit of the specific-factor model, we make the following assumptions. First, we assume away any skill formation or on-job training for the unskilled workers to perform the production activities in the manufacturing sector. We shall consider such possibilities later in Chapter 9. On the other hand, suppose price configurations are such that the skilled wage is always at a premium over the unskilled wage. Thus, whereas unskilled workers would not get any job in the manufacturing sector, there would be no incentive for skilled workers to move into the agriculture.

Along the spirit of the HO theorem, on the other hand, suppose the South, or the home country, exports the agricultural good (X) and imports the manufacturing good (Y). We begin with an initial situation where trade had already taken place between the North and the South, but such trade was restricted by an ad-valorem Southern tariff, t, on imports from the North. The price of imports in the South, P_Y, thus deviates from the world price, $\overline{P_Y}$, by the tariff wedge, $t\overline{P_Y}$. But price of exportables in the South, P_X, and both the domestic prices in the North equal the respective world prices. The competitive profit conditions in the South under such circumstances can be written as,

$$P_X = \overline{P}_X = a_{LX}W + a_{KX}r \tag{3.10}$$

$$P_Y = (1+t)\overline{P}_Y = a_{SY}W_S + a_{KY}r \tag{3.11}$$

where r is the domestic rate of return to capital. The assumed constant and unit exchange rate enables us to quote the world prices in units of home currency.

Two comments are warranted at this point. First, for any given Southern tariff rate, the factor prices there can no longer be determined uniquely by these

---

[15] The specific-factor model is often looked at as a short run variant of the HOS model by interpreting sector-specificity as sectoral immobility of capital in the short run [Mayer (1974), Mussa (1974)]. From a purely academic viewpoint, our specification may similarly be interpreted as long as the underlying time frame is sufficiently long to make capital sectorally mobile but not long enough to transform unskilled workers into skilled ones through education and/or training.

competitive profit conditions at the post-trade equilibrium. The endowment base of the country now influences factor prices. Second, to ensure full employment of all the three factors of production,

$$\overline{L} = a_{LX} X \tag{3.12}$$

$$\overline{S} = a_{SY} Y \tag{3.13}$$

$$\overline{K} = a_{KX} X + a_{KY} Y \tag{3.14}$$

we must assume flexible input coefficients and given the cost-minimization objective underlying the input choices, this is described by the following conditions :

$$a_{iX} = a_{iX}(W, r) \tag{3.15}$$

$$a_{ij} = a_{ij}(W_S, W) \tag{3.16}$$

Similar conditions hold in the North except that $P_Y^* = \overline{P}_Y$.

What would be the effect of trade liberalization by the South (a tariff cut in this set up) on the wage-gap between skilled and unskilled labour there? If the South is a large country, such a policy change will first of all affect the world prices. Lowering of the Southern tariff makes imports cheaper in the South thereby encouraging Southern consumers to consume more of the importable good Y and less of the exportable good X. The relative demand for importables, therefore, increases in the South. As long as tastes are homothetic, changes in real income brought about by trade liberalization do not affect relative demand.}. In the North, on the other hand, at the initial set of world prices there should not be any change in relative demand. Consequently, if the South is large, the world relative demand for good Y will increase (with a corresponding decrease in the world relative demand for good X). The world markets now must be cleared at a higher price of good Y and lower price of good Y. Therefore, tariff cut by the South, moves the terms of trade against the South. However, it is a well-known result of the trade theory that unless Southern import demand is too inelastic, the tariff inclusive domestic price of importables in the South will fall with the tariff reduction[16]. Thus, $\hat{P}_Y < \hat{P}_X < 0$.

The domestic producers respond to this decline in the domestic relative price of importables by expanding the production of exportables and reducing that of importables. Since skilled workers are specific in the sector producing

---

[16] In the literature it is known as the non-Metzler case whereby the direct effect of tariff dominates the terms-of-trade effect.

importables, and were initially fully employed, their money wage unambiguously declines. Competitive forces then require that the rate of return to capital must fall as evident from (3.10). But such fall in rate of return may not necessitate an increase in the unskilled money wage to maintain the other zero-profit condition (3.11) since the price of good X declines as well. Whether unskilled-wage increases or decreases now depends on the value of capital share in this sector (see appendix). Smaller is the capital share, more likely is that the unskilled-wage falls. However, even if so, by the price magnification effect it cannot decline more than the skilled-wage does :

$$0 > \hat{W} > \hat{P}_X > \hat{r} > \hat{P}_Y > \hat{W}_S \tag{3.17}$$

Note that this result is independent of any factor intensity condition. But the excluded-middle phenomenon implied in the SS result (3.7) no longer holds here because the percentage change in rate of return to capital is trapped between the two price changes. The change in real return to the mobile factor, here, capital, is therefore ambiguous. However, the wage-gap unambiguously declines and this is at variance with what we observe in the South.

In the North, on the other hand, since the domestic and the world prices are the same, and the terms of trade moves in its favour, the price magnification effect implies widening of the wage-gap, with change in the rate of return to capital now being ambiguous,

$$\hat{W}_S^* > \hat{P}_Y^* > \hat{r}^* > \hat{P}_X^* > \hat{W}^* \tag{3.18}$$

Thus, once again the standard price magnification effects predict asymmetric changes in the wage-gap.

3.3.2 South Exporting Skill-Intensive Good

The effect of trade liberalization on wages in South changes significantly if we assume that skilled labour is specific in the export sector. One might wonder whether this assumption of skilled labour being specific in export sector in the South is consistent with HOS trade pattern. Whereas in a two-commodity case, this might appear to be a violation of HOS trade pattern, in a many-commodity setting, this is quite plausible. In a recent paper Jones, Beladi and Marjit (1999) argue that a broader interpretation of the HOS theory has to be in the context of a many commodity world. A country *will* export goods consistent with its resource endowments and *will* import goods that are not consistent with the composition of its endowments. A moderately skill-abundant country can import highly skilled and highly unskilled labour-intensive products. In fact, the assumption that South is exporting skill-intensive good is not at variance with the export baskets of quite a few developing countries in recent times. India's increasing share in world markets for software and information technology is a glaring example. There are other examples of Southern countries exporting non-traditional skill-intensive manufactures along with traditional unskilled labour-intensive agricultural goods.

In this case, following the logic of sub-section 3.3.1, a tariff cut leads to the following changes in factor prices[17] :

$$0 > \hat{W}_S > \hat{P}_X > \hat{r} > \hat{P}_Y > \hat{W} \tag{3.19}$$

$$\hat{W}^* > \hat{P}_Y^* > \hat{r}^* > 0 > \hat{P}_X^* > \hat{W}_S^* \tag{3.20}$$

Therefore, the standard model explains the phenomenon of widening wage-gap in the South following trade liberalization when the exportables use sector-specific skilled labour and importables use sector-specific unskilled labour with the capital moving around. But, wage changes in the North are at odds with the empirical findings. Furthermore, once again we have asymmetric changes in the wage-gap in the two countries. However, the above result points to the need of a disaggregative approach in modeling the export sectors in the South taking into account the increasing growth of non-traditional skilled-manufactures in its total exports. But this is only halfway through. The specific-factor model needs to be modified further to generate the symmetry result.

3.4 Conclusion

As evident from the above discussions, the straightjacket application of the Stolper-Samuelson theorem in the context of the standard HOS model or its Specific-factor variants cannot explain the widening wage-gap phenomena observed in most of the Southern countries as well as in the North. The assumption that skilled labour is specific in Southern exportables whereas unskilled labour is specific in production of importables, on the other hand, provides us a setting that generates the income distribution effect in the South similar to what we observe. But it fails to explain the symmetric wage movements in both the countries.

However, this somewhat tailor-made specification of the production structure points more to the necessity of disaggregation of the Southern export sector in line with the recent trends. An appropriate approach towards explaining the widening wage-gap in the South, therefore, should be to incorporate into the basic theoretical framework the asymmetries in the factor intensities in different export sectors, not just across the export and import sectors as in the traditional trade

---

[17] Now the Southern skilled wage and the Northern rate of return to capital may fall or increase.

models, as well as the asymmetries in the wage-formation process and other labour market characteristics prevalent in the South.

APPENDIX

I. The Stolper-Samuelson Theorem

Let $(\hat{P}_X - \hat{P}_Y) > 0$ be the price changes consistent with the rise in home relative price from the autarkic level p_a to the free trade equilibrium price $\bar{p}$. Totally differentiating the zero profit conditions (3.1) and (3.2) in the text we obtain :

$$\hat{P}_X = \theta_{SX}\hat{W}_S + \theta_{LX}\hat{W} \tag{A.3.1}$$

$$\hat{P}_Y = \theta_{SY}\hat{W}_S + \theta_{LY}\hat{W} \tag{A.3.2}$$

where θ_{ij} is the (unit) cost share of i-th input in j-th sector and $\sum_i \theta_{ij} = 1$. .

Thus, the commodity price changes following free trade are the weighted averages of the consequent factor price changes. Subtraction of (A.3.2) from (A.3.1) yields :

$$\hat{P}_X - \hat{P}_Y = (\theta_{SX} - \theta_{SY})\hat{W}_S + (\theta_{LX} - \theta_{LY})\hat{W} \tag{A.3.3}$$

But following Jones (1965),

$$|\theta| = \theta_{SX}\theta_{LY} - \theta_{LX}\theta_{SY}$$
$$= \theta_{SX} - \theta_{SY}$$
$$= \theta_{LX} - \theta_{LY} \qquad [\text{using } \sum_i \theta_{ij} = 1]$$

Therefore, (A.3.3) boils down to,

$$\hat{W}_S - \hat{W} = \frac{\hat{P}_X - \hat{P}_Y}{|\theta|} \tag{A.3.4}$$

Since $|\theta|$ is less than unity in value so (A.3.4) implies a price magnification effect whereby the (absolute) change in skilled wage relative to unskilled wage, $|\hat{W}_S - \hat{W}|$, is more than proportionate to the (absolute) change in relative commodity price, $|\hat{P}_X - \hat{P}_Y|$. Now given that exportables good X is relatively labour-intensive, $|\theta| < 0$, the unskilled money wage increases whereas the skilled wage falls.

II. Price Magnification Effect in the Specific-Factor Model

Consider the percentage change form of the capital constraint (3.14) :

$$0 = \lambda_{KX} (\hat{X} + \hat{a}_{KX}) + \lambda_{KY} (\hat{Y} + \hat{a}_{KY}) \tag{A.3.5}$$

where $\lambda_{Kj} \equiv \dfrac{a_{Kj} X_j}{K}$ is the employment share of capital in j-th sector.

Solving for the output changes from the percentage change forms of (3.12) and (3.13) and substituting the values in (A.3.5) we get,

$$0 = \lambda_{KX} (\hat{a}_{KX} - \hat{a}_{LX}) + \lambda_{KY} (\hat{a}_{KY} - \hat{a}_{SY}) \tag{A.3.6}$$

Define the elasticity of marginal product of capital in the two sectors as [see Caves, Frankel and Jones (1997)] :

$$\gamma_{KX} = -\frac{(\hat{a}_{KX} - \hat{a}_{LX})}{\hat{r} - \hat{P}_X}$$

$$\gamma_{KY} = -\frac{(\hat{a}_{KY} - \hat{a}_{LY})}{\hat{r} - \hat{P}_Y}$$

Using these definitions, the change in rate of return to capital is determined from (A.3.6) as,

$$\hat{r} = \alpha \hat{P}_X + (1 - \alpha) \hat{P}_Y < 0 \tag{A.3.7}$$

where $\alpha \equiv \lambda_{KX} \gamma_{KX} / (\lambda_{KX} \gamma_{KX} + \lambda_{KY} \gamma_{KY})$.

Now from the percentage change forms of eqs. (3.10) and (3.11), using (A.3.7) and $0 > \hat{P}_X > \hat{P}_Y$, we get,

$$\hat{W} = [\theta_{KX} \alpha (\hat{P}_Y - \hat{P}_X) - (\theta_{KX} \hat{P}_Y - \hat{P}_X)] / \theta_{LX} \tag{A.3.8}$$

$$\hat{W}_S = [\theta_{KX} \alpha (\hat{P}_Y - \hat{P}_X) - (1 - \theta_{KY}) \hat{P}_Y] / \theta_{SY} \tag{A.3.9}$$

Since, $0 > \hat{P}_X > \hat{P}_Y$, so $\hat{W}_S$ is unambiguously negative whereas $\hat{W} < 0$ for a small value of θ_{KX}. But regardless of this, since $\hat{P}_X$ is weighted average of $\hat{W}$ and $\hat{r}$, and $\hat{P}_Y$ is weighted average of $\hat{W}_S$ and $\hat{r}$, we arrive at the price magnification effect stated in (3.17) in the text.

4 TRADE LIBERALIZATION AND SYMMETRIC WAGE-GAP

4.1 Two Cases

From the above discussions it is clear that in the standard 2x2x2 HOS framework or its specific-factor variant, trade liberalization must affect the wage-gap asymmetrically in the North and South. Only when endowment differences across the nations are significant and technology exhibits factor intensity reversal, can we expect symmetric changes in the wage-gap as is empirically observed. But this is only a special case. Extension of the basic model to more than two factors of production also cannot explain the widening wage-gap phenomenon.

There are, however, two interesting cases, one in the multiple-good setting of the HOS model with fewer factors of production, and the other in the specific-factor model with a rigidity of unskilled money wage, that generate the desired result. The important factor driving the result in the first case, as we will see shortly, is not the particular type of technology (as in case of factor intensity reversal) but the particular type of trade pattern. At the same time the framework can be used to explain asymmetric wage movements following trade liberalization among the Southern countries. This is demonstrated by Davis (1996) for small price-taking Southern countries. Whereas symmetric changes in wage inequality in both North and South follow from the *local* factor intensity ranking, the asymmetric effect across the Southern countries follows from *local* factor abundance as defined later.

4.2 Generalized HOS Model, Trade Pattern and the Wage-Gap

4.2.1 A Generalized HOS Model

Consider two countries completely specialized in one good each and producing another good in common. Suppose the good produced by both is the *middle-good* in the intensity ranking and is exported by the country that is completely specialized in the good at the bottom of the ranking (i.e., with lowest value of *l*). Both the countries consume all the three goods. Thus, they each export the good in which they specialize completely. We, therefore, have a trade pattern where both the countries export the relatively skill-intensive commodity when compared with the other good they produce. Under such circumstances, reduction of the tariff on the middle-good might lead to widening wage-gap in both countries.

Interestingly, in a three good-two factors of production setting such trade pattern is not an exception but a rule. This has been well demonstrated by Jones (1979). The basic idea is that with goods outnumbering the primary factors of production, a competitive trading economy will produce much fewer goods than it will consume. This is likely to prevail under condition of free trade and for an economy which is small enough to escape the burden of producing anything under the sun. In a world with many goods and skilled and unskilled labour as the only factors of production, free trade will allow the economy to produce at most two goods. Given the international commodity prices, the factor prices will be determined in such a way as to provide the *best* return to each factor and a competitive equilibrium will select the sectors which promises such best returns. If skilled and unskilled labour are employed in productions of X and Y in an economy that can produce X, Y and Z, then it must be the case that the average cost of producing good-Z at the existing factor prices exceeds the world price of Z.

Given the technology, by the standard neo-classical assumption we can uniquely solve for two factor prices from two commodity prices. The free trade configuration of outputs is then to find out either the best pair yielding highest returns or the single sector not promising to do so. To illustrate, let C_X, C_Y and C_Z represent the average cost functions. Then the following equalities, describing zero-profit conditions, must hold if all goods have to be produced :

$$C_j(W_S, W) = P_j, \; j = X, Y, Z \tag{4.1}$$

If we solve for (W_S, W) from zero-profit conditions in sectors X and Y, the average cost for good-Z is determined immediately. With P_Z given exogenously for this small open economy, there is no reason why the equality in (4.1) will hold for good-Z. If $C_Z(W_S, W) > P_Z$, output of Z will be zero. For the opposite inequality, either of X and Y must not be produced at the competitive equilibrium. In general, a small open economy will import a lot of goods and produce a few, equal to or less than the number of primary factors of production.

It is natural to ask which ones to produce. This will be determined by the relative endowment of skilled and unskilled labour. Consider Figure 4.1 where we rank X, Y, Z in terms of factor intensities. Good Z is the most intensive in use of skilled labour whereas good X is most intensive in use of unskilled labour. Note that l_X, l_Y and l_Z are the skilled-unskilled labour ratios employed in the three sectors that depend on the factor and commodity prices. Let North be relatively abundant in skilled labour and the South in unskilled labour. As is exhibited in the Figure, suppose the endowment points of the North and the South, E_N and E_S respectively, do not belong to the same cone of diversification but are different enough for the North to produce goods Z and Y and the South to produce goods Y and X. But they are also not too different so as to allow either of these nations to specialize completely in one of the goods.

Typically, the standard treatment of HOS theory in a 2x2 world with, say, goods Z and Y, will assume the endowments lie in the diversification cone $l_Z O l_Y$ so that both produce both these goods. In this typical scenario restricted trade will mean different prices in different countries. However, if l_Z and l_Y denote fixed-coefficient technology, such price differences will not mean different cones of diversification for different countries. As tariff is removed from Y in the North which it should import from the South (given the HO pattern of trade), it becomes more rewarding to raise the production of good Z in the North that causes a fall in the relative wage of the unskilled workers. In the South, as production of good Y is more lucrative, unskilled workers find their wages relative to the skilled workers going up. Although we have asymmetric effect of trade liberalization in the standard HOS structure demonstrated earlier, in the generalized HOS, trade liberalization has a symmetric effect on wage inequality.

4.2.2 Trade Pattern and Symmetric Effect on Wages

Though trade liberalization has a symmetric effect on wages, whether it raises or reduces the wage-gap depends on the trade pattern. Note that the assumed endowment patterns and the consequent production structures suggest that good Z will be exported by North and good X will be exported by South. In addition, assume that South also exports good Y to North. With an initial tariff on good Y in North, the local price there is given by,

$$P_Y^N = (1+t)P_Y^*(t) \qquad (4.2)$$

where P_Y^* is the price ruling in the world market that depends, inter alia, on Northern tariff rate given the case of two large trading partners.

In South, good Y is sold at the world price :

$$P_Y^S = P_Y^*(t) \qquad (4.3)$$

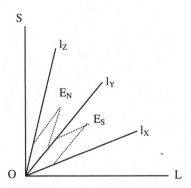

Figure 4.1: Pattern of Trade in a
Generalized HOS Model

Now a reduction of tariff in North raises the import demand for Y causing an increase in world price. Given the price of good X, such increase in P_Y^* shifts production away from good X to good Y in South and following the SS argument the skilled wage relative to the unskilled wage must increase since good Y is relatively skilled-labour intensive there.

On the other hand, it is a well-known result of trade theory that a lowering of tariffs usually lowers the local price of the imported good. Therefore, in the North, production will switch in favour of the good Z and that being skilled-labour intensive compared to good Y, the skilled wage relative to the unskilled wage rises.

If good-Y is imported by South, replicating the above argument, we can verify that trade liberalization by South will reduce the wage-gap in both North and South. Thus, the many commodity case with fewer factors of production and significantly different endowments of the trading nations seem to produce the symmetric effects of trade liberalization on wages.

These possibilities arise because compared to the "rest-of-the-goods", the commodity in question whose trade is being promoted through trade liberalization is skilled-labour intensive in the South but unskilled-labour intensive in the North. This may sound as a case of factor intensity reversal, but there is more to it. Since good X and good Z are quite different, good Y becomes *more* skilled in the South and *less* skilled in the North and this makes it a different case altogether from the factor intensity reversal scenario presented earlier. In other words, even with the unique ranking of X, Y, and Z, in the different cones of diversification for the two countries good Y has different rankings. These are rankings in the local sense that is relevant for effects on wages and crucially differentiates this case from the usual (global) factor intensity reversal case.

So far we have been silent on the general equilibrium outcome in terms of the changes in relative prices. Since there are three goods we have to worry about two relative prices. Note that our result goes through if the price of Y relative to that of Z falls in the North and price of Y relative to that of X rises in South. As the local price of good Y falls in the North, production of Z must increase at its initial price. Lowering of Northern tariff on good Y raises Southern real income whereas as in North it does so if the initial tariff was higher than the *optimal* tariff. Under reasonable assumptions on the demand function for Z, though real income changes raise demand, it is likely that an excess supply of Z in the world market will be generated. Accordingly, the world price of Z falls. If the tariff was not too high, a decline in the tariff will cause real income in North to fall and that in South to increase. This reinforces the excess supply story and hence price of Z declines. In any case, can it decline more than the fall in the local price of good Y in North? Possibly not because in such a case with *relative* price of good Z declining in the

North, the initial boost in supply of Z could not have taken place. This is a stability argument that sustains the case for rising wage-gap in the North.

In the South we have greater production of Y whereas the production of X suffers as the world price of Y faced by the Southern exporters goes up following the lowering of the Northern tariff. But again the chance is bleak that relative price of Y will fall in the South if the excess demand for X is caused by an initial expansion of Y which must hold in equilibrium. The demand for X tends to go up also due to the rise in global real income as free trade yields maximum real income. All said and done, one can clearly conceive of cases where relative price of good Y goes up in the South and down in the North setting the stage for symmetric changes in the wage-gap in the two trading nations.

4.2.3 Is the Trade Pattern Consistent?

It is not difficult to justify the above pattern of trade between the North and the South since there is substantial empirical evidence that the LDCs tend to export a large variety of physical as well as human capital-intensive goods along with primary exports. But the assumption that the trading nations must produce one good in common, the middle-good in the intensity ranking in particular, is rather strong. However, the result goes through if there are goods that are *similar* in nature and not necessarily perfect substitutes.

Does our story violate the HOS theory in the sense that we allow the South to export a skill intensive good? Not necessarily. Once again echoing Jones, Beladi and Marjit (1999) we argue that a broader interpretation of the HOS theory has to be in the context of a many commodity world. A country will export goods consistent with its resource endowments. A country therefore can export labour-intensive as well as skill-intensive goods relative to its endowment pattern. A moderately skill-abundant country can import highly skilled and highly unskilled labour-intensive products. All these are perfectly consistent with the HOS theory in a many commodity world. A phenomena such as the Leontief paradox ceases to be a paradox if one takes such a general view. In fact, if the endowment line for South, E_S, is sufficiently close to the l_Y-line and that of North, E_N, is close to the l_Z-line, we can expect the South to produce lot of good Y and North to produce little of this (and great deal of good Z). In such a case the desired pattern of trade emerges in which the South exports good Y to the North.

Essentially, South still exports the good that is relatively less skill-intensive in the *global* sense. Accordingly, the pattern of trade is not inconsistent with such global ranking. However, what is relevant here and is driving our result is factor intensity ranking in the *local* sense. This is the ranking of goods within the relevant cone of diversification. With different cones of diversification for North and South due to their very asymmetric endowments patterns, the same good Y has *different local intensity ranking though unique global ranking*. Due to such different local intensity rankings, despite asymmetric movements in commodity prices following trade liberalization, effects on wages are identical in both the trading nations.

4.3 Local Factor Abundance and Asymmetric Changes in Wages in the South

The generalized HOS model is also useful in generating the asymmetric factor price movements across similar and unskilled labour abundant Southern countries. Davis (1996) illustrated this for small Southern countries whose endowment rays lie within the same cone of diversification l_YOl_X. Even if all such countries produce the same set of goods Y and X, their trade patterns vary depending on their relative factor abundance *within* this cone of diversification. In Figure 4.2, the Southern countries in region A are most skilled-labour abundant and they produce great deal of Y but little of X. The least skilled-labour countries are those in region A' and their export patterns and that of countries in region A are *complementary*. On the other hand, those countries in region M are at an intermediate level of skilled-labour abundance and satisfy their own needs for both Y and X. Thus they export both these goods for Z. The crucial point to note is that all the Southern countries are relatively unskilled-labour abundant in global sense but have different *local factor abundance*. And for the effect of trade liberalization in each of these *different* Southern countries, it is these local factor abundances that are relevant.

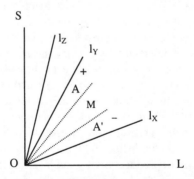

Figure 4.2: Local Factor Abundance
and Wage-Gap in the South

Assume that each Southern country initially has imposed an ad-valorem tariff on their respective import items. Consider first a representative country in region A. For such a country, a reduction of tariffs on the imported good X lowers its price there and accordingly raises the return to the *locally abundant* skilled labour relative to that of the *locally scarce* unskilled labour. That is, the wage-gap increases. This happens despite the fact that this country is a skilled labour scarce Southern country in the global sense. Note that since this country is small, trade liberalization there does not affect factor prices in the other Southern countries.

Replicating this argument it is straightforward to check that a reduction of tariffs on imports of Y by a representative country in region A' will reduce the return to the locally scarce skilled labour and raise that to the unskilled labour that is locally abundant.

4.4 Rigid-Wage Specific-Factor Model

Often in the LDCs as well as in many parts of Europe the minimum wage laws are in force. Sometimes the money wages are contractual that prohibits any movement in the wages following a terms of trade change. In India, for example, the money wages for unskilled and semi-skilled workers are often set by the tripartite agreements between the government, the management and the labour union. Such wages are kept fixed for a certain period of time and then revised upward. Once such fixity of unskilled money wage in the South is incorporated in a specific factor model, trade liberalization may widen the wage-gap in both the countries.

Consider the specific-factor setting of the previous chapter : Skilled and unskilled labour are specific to the sectors producing good Y and good X respectively. Good Y is imported by the South and initially such imports were restricted there by an ad-valorem tariff. Now consider a reduction in tariff. To set aside the consequent employment effect, and focus only on the income distribution aspect, we assume that all input coefficients are fixed. This assumption essentially fixes both the output levels and hence the level of employment. The (relative) supply is, therefore, invariant with respect to changes in commodity prices. Recall the competitive profit conditions (3.10) and (3.13) in the South from the previous Chapter. With the unskilled money wage now pegged at a (higher) level $\overline{W}$, the skilled money wage and the rate of return to capital are uniquely determined by the given world prices for any given tariff rate. That is, the flexible factor prices are determined much in the same fashion as in a typical symmetric ($m = n$) HOS model. Since, as spelled out earlier, reduction of the Southern tariff lowers the domestic price of exportables in the South, the rate of return to capital declines given a pegged unskilled money wage. But with the domestic price of importables falling as well, change in the skilled money wage now depends on the factor intensity ranking :

$$\hat{W}_S = \frac{1}{\theta_{SY}} \left[\hat{P}_Y - \frac{\theta_{KY}}{\theta_{KX}} \hat{P}_X \right]$$

(4.4)

Since $0 > \hat{P}_X > \hat{P}_Y$, if the Southern importables are relatively capital intensive ($\theta_{KY} > \theta_{KX}$), the skilled money wage may increase and the wage-gap may widen in the South. With the Northern wage-gap widening as well (see (3.18)), wage movements are symmetric in the two countries.

Thus, a rigid unskilled money wage in a specific-factor setting with more factors than goods ($m < n$) generates the observed effects. As we will demonstrate later, this together with other labour market characteristics prevalent in the South allows for more interesting possibilities.

4.5 Conclusion

The symmetric changes in the wage-gap across the North and the South that have been observed, can be explained in terms of a generalized HOS model where the countries completely specialize in goods that are at the two ends of the intensity ranking and produce in common a *middle* good. Such patterns of production and specialization arise when there are fewer domestic factors of production than the number of traded goods and the endowment patterns of the countries are significantly different. Of course, whether the wage-gap widens or declines in both the countries following trade liberalization depends on who exports this "middle" good. In any case, however, we have symmetric movements in wages. At the same time, following Davis (1996), one can use the framework to explain the asymmetric wage movements in the developing countries of East Asia and Latin-America.

5 INPUT TRADE: AN ALTERNATIVE EXPLANATION

5.1 Introduction

Of late, a few trade theorists have advocated that direct foreign investments, factor flows and trade in intermediate products can be the likely sources of symmetric changes in the wage-gap across the North and South. Markusen and Venables (1996) emphasize the role of multinationals to be more important as they alter the nature of trade from trade in final goods to trade in skill-intensive producer services. That direct foreign investment may explain the wage-gap phenomenon has also been advocated by Feenstra and Hanson (1996, 2001), Lawrence (1994) and Slaughter (1994).

Markusen and Venables consider a 2x2 economy where one sector is composed of three distinct activities : skilled labour creating firm-specific knowledge capital, such as blueprints; skilled labour producing plant-specific capital in combination with unskilled labour; and unskilled labour producing the final good using the plant-specific capital. The location of firm-specific capital determines the nationality of the firm. The multinationals locate skilled labour-intensive activities and one production plant in their home country and one additional plant in the host country. In the case of asymmetric relative endowments but similar country size, entry of multinationals due to removal of investment barrier, raises the wage-gap in the skilled labour abundant country. In the unskilled labour abundant country, on the other hand, the effect on the wage-gap is ambiguous. However, if relative endowments of the two countries are significantly different, a rising wage-gap in both countries is more likely.

The analysis of Feenstra and Hanson (1996), on the other hand, uses a variant of the Dornbusch-Fisher-Samuelson (1977) model where a single manufacturing good is assembled from a continuum of intermediate inputs. Such inputs are produced by skilled labour, unskilled labour and capital. In equilibrium South produces and exports a range of inputs up to some critical ratio of skilled to unskilled labour with the North producing the remainder inputs. In such a context, growth of relative stock of capital in the South will raise the critical ratio dividing the Northern and Southern activities. The activities transferred from the North to the South will be more skilled labour intensive in the South but less skilled labour intensive in the North. Therefore, relative demand for skilled labour increases in both the countries resulting in growing wage inequality in both North and South. This is similar to our middle-good story of the previous chapter. Consider, for example, a substantial increase in skilled labour force in North that pushes its endowment ray outside the cone of diversification $l_Z O l_Y$ (see Figure 4.1). North then specializes completely in the most skill-intensive good Z and the production of the middle-good Y is relocated in South. The wage-gap must widen in both North and South through increase in demand for skilled-labour consequent upon such increases in production of relatively skill-intensive goods: good Z in North and good Y in South.

We here, however, provide a different channel through which trade in intermediate goods lead to growing wage inequality in both North and South. Unlike Feenstra and Hanson (1996), we separate out trade in inputs and capital flow from North to South (or capital growth in South) to demonstrate how liberalization of input trade by itself explains the symmetric wage movements across the globe. However, we take a very traditional model of trade with one homogeneous intermediate good being produced by skilled labour and then the two are combined to produce the manufacturing good. Our purpose is not to set up an innovative model, but drawing out a meaningful mechanism that generates our desired outcome consistent with empirical observations regarding growing wage inequality. Once the basic mechanism is understood, the context which contains such a mechanism can be altered.

In section 5.3, we explore the avenues through which factor flows in a model with no intermediate good may lead to symmetric increasing wage-gap. However, it will be made clear why it is difficult to pin down factor flows per se as a possible culprit behind growing inequality across the globe. While larger capital inflow reduces the cost of capital and tends to raise wages, there is no presumption as to how the wage distribution will behave in the home and host country. A complex pattern of resource flows involves capital outflow from the North and labour outflow from the South. International migration, legal or illegal, of labour with heterogeneous skills will have different implications for intra-country inequality in the structure of wages. This indicates the more important role that trade in intermediates rather than factor flows plays. In exploring these theoretical possibilities we make heavy use of variants of the specific-factor model primarily because it generates incentives for factor flows across the borders.

5.2 Trade in Intermediate Products

5.2.1 A Simple Example

To have an idea how trade in intermediate good can lead to symmetric changes in wages, consider the following simple example. Imagine a world where intermediate products are exported by the North to the South. Initially, such imports were subject to a Southern tariff. Skilled labour is used in the intermediate goods producing sector as well as in the final good sector that uses such an intermediate good. This scenario is not at all at variance with reality and we will later provide examples of some Southern countries where the trade pattern perfectly fits with this. Now, consider trade liberalization in South. As a tariff on the intermediate good is removed in the South, North gains because price of the intermediate good goes up in the world market provided of course the Southern country is a large country in the usual sense. This tends to increase the relative wage of the skilled workers in the North. Absent the Metzler paradox, the price of the intermediate good in the South goes down and thus it is now cheaper to produce the final good. Since this sector uses the skilled labour, competition tends to push up the demand for them and accordingly the skilled-wage goes up in South as well. This rather naive argument indicates that a model that provides a theoretical structure, tying up the loose ends and properly working out the interactions between export and import-competing sectors of course, holds the promise of explaining growing wage inequality in both North and South. Note that unlike in the generalized HOS model discussed in Chapter 4, where the cross-country link in the pattern of wage inequality was established through a good produced in common, the bridge here is built through an intermediate good.

5.2.2 A Simple General Equilibrium Model with Intermediate Good

Let us consider a simple general equilibrium model that captures the above story. Contemplate a trade scenario where the North exports an intermediate good (M) to the South who in turn processes it with skilled labour to produce a final good Y and re-exports it to the North. The computer industry in India best exemplifies the above story. It imports state-of-the-art hardware components and exports processed software involving a lot of skilled labour component. Another example would be India exporting finished gems and jeweler produced by its skilled labour using imported pearls and other precious metals. For analytical purpose, we assume that South does not produce any local prototype of the intermediate good. The requirement of the intermediate good is entirely met through imports. Initially there is a tariff on the import of the intermediate good in the South. Both countries produce another final good X using capital and unskilled labour but relative abundance of unskilled labour in South makes it an exporter of this good. Thus both the final goods are exported by the South whereas the North exports the intermediate good. However, this is quite consistent with the emerging trade pattern of the North in recent times with the improvement of the communications technology across the globe.

Given such production structure and trade pattern, the zero-profit and full-employment conditions in South are as follows :

$$1 = a_{LX}W + a_{KX}r \tag{5.1}$$

$$P_Y = a_{SY}W_S + a_{KY}r + a_{MY}(1+t)P_M(t) \tag{5.2}$$

$$\bar{L} = a_{LX}X \tag{5.3}$$

$$\overline{S} = a_{SY} Y \tag{5.4}$$

$$\overline{K} = a_{KX} X + a_{KY} Y \tag{5.5}$$

Similar conditions specify the production structure in North. The variables for North are marked by asterisk to distinguish them from those for the South. Note that we have measured all prices in terms of good X. The world price of the intermediate good depends, inter alia, on the Southern tariff because of the large country assumption. Also, we assume different production technologies, embodied in the input-coefficients across North and South. Of course, there are the input-choice conditions in South,

$$a_{ij} = a_{ij}(W_S, W, r) \tag{5.6}$$

and similar conditions in North. Finally we have the world-market clearing conditions for final good Y and intermediate good M [18] :

$$D_Y(P_Y, R) + D_Y^*(P_Y^*, R^*) = Y \tag{5.7}$$

$$a_{MY} Y = M^* \tag{5.8}$$

where D_Y is the demand for good Y in South and R is the Southern real income. Note that both the North and the South have the standard specific-factor structures. As has been elaborated in Chapter 3, the solution mechanism for the above system of equations in North and South is pretty straightforward.

We now proceed to analyze the consequences of a drop in southern tariff t on the Southern and Northern wage-ratios. To this end, first of all we need to check the relationship between Southern tariff and domestic and world price of the intermediate good. If we assume away the paradoxes such as Lerner's Case and Metzler Paradox, the reduction of Southern tariff is expected to raise the world price and reduce the domestic price of the intermediate good. It is easy to check the conditions under which such normal outcomes hold. How do such changes in the price of the intermediate good affect wage-distribution in the two countries? In a complete general equilibrium analysis, not only are wages affected directly but also indirectly by the induced change in the world price of the manufacturing good Y that South exports. Let us begin with the direct effect. That is, we ask the following question : What effect on the wage-gaps in the two countries can we expect *at the initial price of good Y* when South reduces its tariff on the import of intermediate good?

---

[18] By Walras' Law, the world market for good X must then automatically be cleared.

Let us begin with the North. It is immediate from the analysis in Chapter 3 that an increase in world price of intermediate good must raise the skilled-wage and reduce the unskilled-wage. With skilled and unskilled workers being specific to the intermediate and manufacturing sectors respectively and both initially fully employed, such changes in wages are the result of increased demand for skilled labour and a fall in demand for unskilled labour. Note that since scarce capital is used in both sectors, the tariff-cut induced expansion of intermediate good production in North is possible only through a fall in production of manufacturing good releasing the required capital. This in turn lowers the demand for unskilled labour used in this sector. Therefore, tariff liberalization by South widens the wage-gap in North at initial price of good Y.

In the South, what is relevant for wage distribution is not the increase in the world price but a fall in the domestic price of the intermediate good, $[1 + t]P_M(t)$. Given the nominal price of good Y, this raises the effective price of it, $P_Y - [1 + t]P_M(t)$. Once again by the price magnification effect in a factor-specific model like this, the skilled-wage must increase and unskilled money wage must fall unambiguously. Therefore, the wage-gap widens in both the countries.

However, the above thought experiment is carried out for a given world price of the manufacturing good Y that uses the intermediate good. How is the above result altered when we allow the price of good Y to change? First of all note that since the cost of producing good Y falls consequent upon reduction of tariff by South on import of Intermediate good, relative (world) price of good Y should fall in the wake of rising supply of good Y in the world market. This eats into the benefit of the skilled workers as evident from the zero-profit condition (5.2). However, it is easy to check the demand conditions where such fall in price of good Y will not be too large to reverse our result. Of course, the increase in world real income due to trade liberalization raises the (world) demand for good Y that mitigates the fall in its price to some extent.

The central message is that with trade in intermediate product, there is sufficient scope for wage inequality to grow across the globe when such trade is liberalized. Such results can be generated even within the context of conventional general equilibrium models provided of course a broader analytical perspective is developed with appropriate basic structure.

5.3   Factor Mobility: How Far Does It Explain?

It is well recognized in the literature on factor mobility and trade that international factor flows tend to equalize factor prices across the globe. Such presumption rests on the assumption of uniform technology and commodity prices in the North and South. But though free commodity trade generates uniform commodity prices, the level of technology can differ across the nations and consequently factors can earn different returns in different countries. Whereas the traditional literature enriched by seminal works of Jones (1967), Kemp (1966) and Mundell (1957) focus on the interaction between trade and factor flows, the issue of international factor movement and income distribution within a country has not received much attention from the theorists. Recent survey of Wong (1995) provides a taxonomy of different results available in the literature emphasizing the role of policies that target national welfare rather than inequality per se. But the recent debate on trade and wage-gap is yet to find its voice in the literature on factor movements. Findlay's (1984) classic survey of the North-South models focus on the relative well being of the North and South following capital flows from the developed to the developing countries. Once again the issue of income distribution takes a back seat because the empirical evidence of the problem emerged only in the late 1980s and early 1990s as the rich nations started experiencing growing income inequality and rising unemployment among the unskilled workers.

An instructive way to understand the implications of factor flows for wage inequality is to use the standard specific-factor model. Such theoretical outcomes may or may not corroborate stylized empirical evidences. However, this can serve as a useful benchmark when one wishes to design a more complex set-up to get nearer to the observed pattern of movement.

Consider the simple structure with mobile physical capital and sector specific labour discussed in Chapter 3. The two goods Y and Z are produced by unskilled and skilled labour respectively with the help of capital that moves across the sectors freely. Assume the usual neo-classical technology and competitive markets. Without rewriting the full structure, we consider the following two equations that are sufficient for our analytical expositions :

$$a_{SZ}W_S + a_{KZ}r = 1 = a_{SZ}^*W_S^* + a_{KZ}^*r^* \tag{5.9}$$

$$a_{LY}W + a_{KY}r = P_Y = a_{LY}^*W^* + a_{KY}^*r^* \tag{5.10}$$

where P_Y is the relative price of good Y. These two are competitive price equations in North and South under free commodity trade. It is well known, however, that free trade will usually not equalize the factor prices in such a framework. As explained earlier, unlike the HOS model, here factor endowments of the two countries will influence the factor prices. As discussed in detail in Jones (1971), a greater stock of capital will reduce its return and raise both the skilled and unskilled wage. It is likely that larger supply of skilled or unskilled labour will work towards a higher return to capital and lower wages. Hence, a country with relatively strong contingent of skilled and/or unskilled labour and a smaller capital base, should have a higher return to capital and lower wages. Since it is reasonable to characterize the North as *relatively* capital abundant, so in pre-factor flow situation we can expect the following factor-price differences :

$$W < W^*, \ W_S < W_S \ and \ r > r^* \tag{5.11}$$

Note that the relationship between factor prices and factor endowments are conditioned by the assumptions regarding technology. If the North has superior technology relative to the South and such an advantage outweighs the impact of capital abundance in the North, the return to capital may well be higher in North than that in the South. However, we set aside such a possibility and assume inequalities in (5.11).

Consider the situation when international factor market opens up and capital is the factor that is allowed to move internationally. Given (5.11), Northern capital will start moving into the South until the returns to capital in the two countries are equalized. Of course, in the new equilibrium, r^* will be higher and r will be lower than before. Consequently, in the South both skilled and unskilled wages will increase and those in the North should fall. Relative wage movement in each country can be calculated as :

$$\hat{W}_S - \hat{W} = -\left[\frac{\theta_{KZ}}{1-\theta_{KZ}} - \frac{\theta_{KY}}{1-\theta_{KY}} \right] \hat{r} \tag{5.12}$$

$$\hat{W}_S^* - \hat{W}^* = -\left[\frac{\theta_{KZ}^*}{1-\theta_{KZ}^*} - \frac{\theta_{KY}^*}{1-\theta_{KY}^*} \right] \hat{r} \tag{5.13}$$

If the sector Z using skilled labour in each country uses capital more intensively relative to the other sector as reflected in $\theta_{KZ} > \theta_{KY}$ and $\theta^*_{KZ} > \theta^*_{KY}$, wage inequality must grow in South but decline in the North. The only way inequality can grow across the globe is through a factor intensity reversal. Since we are comparing similar goods, such an assumption seems to be quite arbitrary.

Does labour migration (of both types) explain symmetric changes in wage inequality? Not necessarily. It is straightforward to check that be it labour or capital, factor mobility implies a rising return to capital in the North. This may happen either through capital outflow to the South or through labour inflow into the North. This process leads to rising wages in the South and falling wages in the North. As argued above such relocation of factors of production leads the wage-gap to increase in the South and drop in the North.

Note that all these results are derived at a given set of commodity prices. As a matter of fact we have not mentioned anything about the international prices of goods after the resources have moved from one country to another. The interesting point is that we do not need to as long as we are interested in the relative wages. We know the direction of the movement of factor prices and it is sufficient to determine the wage-gap. That is why we do not have prices explicitly in the relationship (5.12) and (5.13). Also note that if any one of these factors is allowed to move freely, factor prices will be automatically equalized across the globe provided of course technology is uniform.

5.4 Conclusion

The central message of this chapter is that trade in inputs, a dominant feature of North-South trade, can indeed explain the phenomenon of widening of wage-gap in both North and South. However, this case is not as strong as trade liberalization in a generalized HOS structure discussed in Chapter 4. The international factor mobility, on the other hand, cannot account for the growing inequality everywhere. Ceteris paribus, such factor flows may widen the wage-gap in the South but at the same time lead to a more egalitarian outcome in the North. Thus, whereas one can locate input trade as one plausible explanation of symmetric wage movements across the globe, factor flows does not appear to be an appropriate alternative avenue.

III

TRADE, CAPITAL FLOW AND EMPLOYMENT

6 LIBERALIZATION AND EMPLOYMENT IN THE ORGANIZED SECTOR

6.1 Introduction

In Europe, particularly in Germany, France, Portugal, Spain, Sweden and UK, the deteriorating position of the unskilled workers has been reflected in rising unemployment among them. Similar is the story in many parts of Asia and Latin-America. Referring back to Table 2.11, in Chile, Colombia, Philippines, Spain, Turkey and India, unemployment increased substantially during their respective liberalization episodes. In India, the burden of such trade-induced adjustments is borne mostly by those engaged in agriculture, mining and processed primary manufacturing. There has also been quite a sharp fall in employment in skill-intensive manufacturing sector both in India and China. Part of the reason for such displacement of labour, as is often argued, is the inflexible labour markets where money wages often cannot be adjusted downward to allow the industry to adjust its labour costs to trade-induced shocks.

This chapter reviews the link between trade and investment liberalization and the aggregate employment of a homogeneous workforce that has been discussed in the literature.

6.2 The Existing Literature

The issue of trade and employment dates back to Adam Smith's vent for surplus approach and the subsequent "trade as engine of growth" arguments. After the reshaping of the macroeconomic ideas by Keynes and Kalecki in terms of their effective demand approach during the 1930s, the link between foreign trade and aggregate employment was established from the demand side. Since then the Keynesian framework and its variants have been the dominant undercurrent in analyzing expansionary effect of trade and exchange rate policies. The essence of the argument is that the expansionary effect at constant commodity prices is contingent upon the ability of trade and exchange rate policies to generate an export surplus and consequently raise the effective demand that determines aggregate output and employment[19]. In case of currency devaluation, the famous

---

[19] This was first pointed out by Kalecki (1971) in the context of the controversy between Rosa Luxembourg and Tugan Baranovski on the realization of profits. Export surplus, not just exports, being the component of effective demand for domestic output, any policy can raise employment only if it raises the export surplus. But when commodity prices are

Marshall-Lerner condition that the sum of home and foreign import demand elasticities be greater than unity ensures such an increase in the export surplus, whereas for trade liberalization the requirement is that the home import demand be price inelastic[20, 21].

Though the effective demand framework has been the major framework for analyzing the employment effect of trade and exchange rate policies, dual-economy and the rigid-wage general equilibrium models have been used more often than any other framework. There are two types of dual economy models. One is the structuralist model with fixed-price, excess-capacity industrial sector and flexible-price, full-capacity agricultural sector. This approach, often seen as an extension of the one-sector effective demand model, has been used extensively by Mihir Rakshit (1982), Lance Taylor (1983) and Amit Bhaduri (1986), among others[22]. Recasting the Smithian vent for surplus argument as essentially an effective-demand problem, Acharyya (1994b) demonstrates how opening up of trade leads to utilization of excess capacities and greater employment in both the trading nations. In standard Keynesian model this is not possible because both the nations cannot have export surpluses simultaneously in a two-country world. It is this delinking of the expansionary effect from the requirement of export surplus, similar in spirit of the Laursen-Metzler effect though for quite different reason, that is the essence of such an analysis. However, this is beyond the scope of this book.

The second one in the class of dual economy approaches is the open economy Harris-Todaro model worked on extensively by Khan (1980, 1982), Hazari and Sgro (1991), Hazari, Jayasuriya and Sgro (1992), Chao and Yu (1993), Gupta (1994, 1995) and Beladi and Marjit (1996). In section 6.3 we briefly look into the basic model and how it links trade with unemployment drawing heavily from Beladi and Marjit (1996).

The other approach we elaborate on in this chapter is the rigid-wage general equilibrium model and its dependent-economy variants. The important distinction to be made in this context is between the real-wage and money-wage rigidity, on the one hand, and between wage rigidity affecting aggregate employment directly by altering factor proportions (as in specific-factor model) and indirectly through change in demand for the non-traded good.

---

flexible, output and employment can expand even with unchanged trade balance position through what is known as the Laursen-Metzler effect.

[20] See Dornbusch (1980) for a textbook exposition of these relationships.

[21] The important pre-condition is, of course, initial balanced trade. Otherwise a contractionary effect is more likely. This may also work through other channels as demonstrated by Cooper (1971), Diaz-Alejandro (1963) and Krugman and Taylor (1978).

[22] An earlier work in this regard was done by Arup Mallik (1977). The model developed by Amitava Bose (1989) also deserves attention.

However, most of these analyses consider aggregate employment of the homogeneous workforce. No distinction is made between skilled and unskilled workforce and how trade changes employment of these groups that are more relevant in the context of the present book. More importantly, even though these analyses can indicate how employment opportunities for unskilled workers change, with which we are particularly concerned after all, these models can throw little light on the actual employment scenario unless reinterpreted carefully, because no distinction is made between organized and unorganized sector employment. That is, these are primarily the analyses of organized sector employment[23]. But as pointed out earlier, between 60 - 90 percent of total employment in the developing countries are in the unorganized sectors. These models, therefore, can capture only a small part of the impact of trade on aggregate employment of even unskilled workers. However, despite such limitations one must understand how trade is expected to affect such aggregate employment in the organized sectors in a standard framework before extending it to the case of segmented labour markets. After all, these results at least can indicate how trade and investment liberalization are expected to allocate unskilled labour across the organized and unorganized sectors.

This is the perspective from which the present chapter should be viewed. Two particular issues are taken up for analysis. First is how tariff or trade liberalization affects aggregate (organized) employment. There is the general apprehension that as imports displaces domestic import-competing production, with downward rigidity of wages, aggregate employment must fall. But Beladi and Marjit (1996) show that on the contrary, in a typical Harris-Todaro dual economy framework, lowering of tariff may in fact raise aggregate employment. Section 6.2 deals with this. However, as will be demonstrated in section 6.3, in a general equilibrium framework, with or without non-traded production, the general apprehension turns out to be the actuality when wages are rigid in money terms.

The second issue that we address is how foreign investment affects aggregate employment. Interestingly, regardless of the destination of such investment, it appears to be expansionary in a wider set of frameworks compared to trade liberalization.

6.3 Tariff, Foreign Investment and Employment in a Dual Economy

Efficiency of tariff protection in generating higher employment should depend on the labour-intensity of a sector. In a typical two-sector model with specific factors and unemployed labour available at a given money wage, the share of each sector in employment is a crucial factor along with technical parameters.

---

[23] The notable exception, of course, is that of Hazari, Jayasuriya and Sgro (1992).

But Beladi and Marjit (1996) develop a simple Harris-Todaro model in the tradition of Hazari and Sgro (1991) and Khan (1980, 1982) to demonstrate that tariff protection to the urban manufacturing sector might reduce employment independent of any intensity ranking. This means that trade liberalization, under certain circumstances is employment generating contrary to popular perception. On the other hand, in a similar framework, Marjit, Broll and Mitra (1997) establish a rather strong result: Foreign capital inflow, regardless of its destination, unambiguously reduces aggregate employment.

6.3.1 Trade Liberalization and Employment

Consider the standard Harris-Todaro characterization of a dual economy : The urban industrial sector of the economy offering higher institutionally given money wage, $\overline{W}$ and the rural agricultural sector paying lower market-determined money wage, W, to the workers. These two wages are related through the migration equilibrium condition requiring that the expected urban wage must be equal to the rural wage. In the urban sector a manufacturing good Y and an intermediate good M are produced by combining labour (L) and capital (K). In the rural sector, the agricultural good X is produced using labour and the intermediate good. Thus there is a backward linkage between industry and agriculture.

Suppose the economy exports good X and imports good Y that is quite consistent with the overall trade pattern of the developing countries particularly during the early stages of their development. The economy is small and thus faces given set of world commodity prices $\left(P_X^*, P_Y^*\right)$. The intermediate good is not traded and consequently its market must clear domestically. Given such prices, perfect competition should imply following zero-profit conditions :

$$P_X^* = a_{LX}W + a_{MX}P_M \tag{6.1}$$

$$(1+t)P_Y^* = a_{LY}\overline{W} + a_{KY}r \tag{6.2}$$

$$P_M = a_{LM}\overline{W} + a_{KM}r \tag{6.3}$$

where t is the ad-valorem tariff rate.

The domestic capital is fully employed,

$$\overline{K} = a_{KM}M + a_{KY}Y \tag{6.4}$$

But in a typical Harris-Todaro model like this, labour in the urban sector is not fully employed due to a rigid money wage. Such unemployment persists, despite availability of jobs in the rural sector, because these unemployed, who were attracted by the higher urban wage but did not find the job, hang around in the urban sector for better luck next time. Though this typical assumption is questionable and recent empirical evidence shows on the contrary that poor people are too poor to afford such a luxury of remaining jobless, let us continue with this assumption. Thus, if L_e denotes aggregate employment,

$$\overline{L} > L_e = a_{LM} M + a_{LX} X + a_{LY} Y \tag{6.5}$$

The allocation of the total labour force across the urban and rural sectors is given by the migration equilibrium condition :

$$\left[\frac{a_{LY} Y + a_{LM} M}{\overline{L} - a_{LX} X} \right] \overline{W} = W \tag{6.6}$$

Note that, for any given X, $(\overline{L} - a_{LX} X)$ are the job seekers in the urban sector of which only $(a_{LY} Y + a_{LM} M)$ number of people can be absorbed given Y and M. Thus the term in the parenthesis in (6.6) defines the probability of getting an urban job and consequently the left hand side expression gives us the *expected* urban wage. Workers migrate from rural to urban sector till this expected wage rate is equalized with the rural wage.

Finally, we have the domestic market-clearing condition for the non-traded intermediate good M :

$$a_{MX} X = M \tag{6.7}$$

Let us now look at how the output levels, aggregate employment and factor prices are determined. First of all, note that given the ad-valorem tariff and commodity prices, zero-profit conditions (6.1) - (6.3) together determine the rural wage, the rate of return to capital and the domestic price of the intermediate good. The interesting observation at this point is that just like the typical HOS model, the factor prices are determined independent of their respective market-clearing conditions. Of course, had the urban wage not been given institutionally, such one-to-one correspondence would not hold.

The market for intermediate good being entirely domestic, it cannot be produced in excess of what is demanded. Thus, (6.7) determines the output of intermediate good for a given X. Substitution of such a value in (6.6) then yields combination of final good output levels consistent with the migration equilibrium:

$$\frac{W}{\overline{W}} \overline{L} = a_{LY} Y + (a_{LM} a_{MX} + \frac{W}{\overline{W}} a_{LX}) X \tag{6.6a}$$

Similarly, using (6.7), the full employment condition for domestic capital (6.4) can be written as,

$$\overline{K} = a_{KM}a_{MX}X + a_{KY}Y \qquad (6.4a)$$

This states that the direct and indirect requirement of capital in the final traded sectors must exhaust total stock of capital. The conditions (6.4a) and (6.6a) together then determine the output levels of the final traded goods.

Figure 6.1 illustrates the output equilibrium with aggregate unemployment. The line MM' is the locus of X and Y that satisfies (6.6a). The line KK' is, on the other hand, the locus of X and Y consistent with full employment of capital. This constraint is drawn flatter than MM' on the assumption that,

$$\frac{a_{MX}a_{KM}}{a_{KY}} < \frac{a_{LM}a_{MX}}{a_{LY}} + \frac{W}{\overline{W}}\frac{a_{LX}}{a_{LY}} \qquad (6.8)$$

This condition essentially means that good X is labour intensive in direct and indirect sense relative to good Y.

For a given set of commodity prices and tariff, and consequent rural wage, the equilibrium is obtained at point E_o with corresponding output levels as X_o and Y_o. Had there been full employment of labour, from (6.5) with $\overline{L} = L_e$, we would have,

$$\overline{L} = a_{LY}Y + (a_{LM}a_{MX} + a_{LX})X \qquad (6.9)$$

The full employment of labour line LL', representing (6.9), should be at the right of point E_o. As long as $\overline{W} > W$, the full employment line lies wholly to the right of

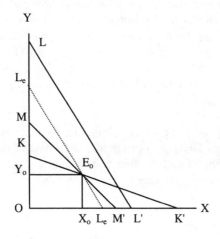

Figure 6.1: Output and Unemployment when
Good X is Relatively Labour-Intensive

and is steeper than the migration-equilibrium line MM′. Moreover, this line is drawn even steeper than the KK′ line. In Figure 6.2 we depict the other relevant case where KK′ is steeper than LL′. The full employment equilibrium is shown by the point E. The broken line through E_o, parallel to LL′ indicates the level of employment with the distance from the LL′ line measuring the extent of unemployment.

How does a reduction in tariffs affect this aggregate employment? To examine let us begin with the fixed coefficient case. From Figure 6.1, it follows that with the positions of LL′ and KK′ thus fixed, the tariff cut raises aggregate employment if the equilibrium changes towards point E along KK′. This is possible if rural wage increases which shifts MM′ to the right and makes it steeper as well. This is, however, indeed the case. For a given set of world prices, the tariff cut lowers the domestic price of imports. With the money wage fixed in the import-competing sector, the entire burden of such a price fall is borne by capital through a fall in its rate of return. This lowers the capital cost of producing the intermediate good and consequently its cost-determined price. With the world price of the agricultural good not changing, the savings on average cost of intermediate good there is matched by corresponding increase in the money wage.

Does this result depend on KK′ being flatter than MM′, i.e., on (6.8)? Figure 6.2 illustrates that condition (6.8) is not a necessary condition. Note that, to avoid complete specialization we must make KK′ line steeper than LL′ as well, i.e., must assume that agricultural exports are relatively intensive in their (indirect) requirement of capital. However, once again increase in the rural wage ensures that aggregate employment increases.

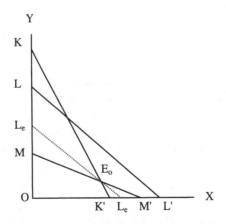

Figure 6.2: Good X is Relatively Capital-Intensive

It might appear that tariff liberalization unambiguously raises aggregate employment. But this is certainly not the case. What Figures 6.1 and 6.2 suggest is that the condition underlying the expansionary effect is not just related to relative capital intensities of the final traded sectors. To derive the exact condition, we proceed as follows.

The tariff cut causes production of urban manufacturing import-competing good (Y) to contract, which releases a_{LY} units of labour and a_{KY} units of capital per unit of output. The latter makes possible a_{KY}/a_{KM} units of additional production of the intermediate good requiring $a_{KY}a_{LM}/a_{KM}$ units of additional labour. On the other hand, as the rural wage increases, agricultural activity becomes attractive. Workers move to rural sector and agricultural production expands. At this point it is important to realize that the increase in the rural wage is a necessary condition for employment expansion. The intermediate good being non-traded, its output is determined by demand generating from agriculture. If the rural wage had fallen after the tariff cut, agricultural activity, and consequently the demand for the intermediate good, would have fallen through migration of workers towards the urban sector. This would have caused more unemployment there. The wage increase rules this out and creates the scope for employment expansion through reverse migration. But, given that workers move to agriculture now, to absorb all the additional production of the intermediate good and to maintain full employment of capital, how much must the agricultural production expand? Since increase in the supply of the intermediate good to absorb all capital released by the contracting Y-sector must equal a_{KY}/a_{KM}, so the required expansion of agricultural output must be $a_{KY}/a_{KM}a_{MX}$. This employs additional labour by the amount $a_{KY}a_{LX}/a_{KM}a_{MX}$. Thus aggregate employment increases if

$$\frac{a_{LX}}{a_{MX}a_{KM}} + \frac{a_{LM}}{a_{KM}} > \frac{a_{LY}}{a_{KY}} \qquad (6.10)$$

Note that, if the intermediate good is labour intensive relative to the imported manufacturing good, this condition is satisfied and hence the employment expansion following trade liberalization is ensured[24]. This is obvious because this means that the expanding M-sector absorbs more labour than is released by the Y-sector so that urban employment increases. With agricultural production expanding as well due to the reverse migration following the wage increase, such a fall in urban unemployment means a decline in the total unemployment [25]. Therefore,

---

[24] Had there been no wage differential, this would boil down to condition (6.8). Only in such a case, for an employment expansion we would have required that the agricultural good is labour intensive (in direct and indirect sense) relative to the manufacturing good.
[25] Such reverse migration is quite consistent with observations in India [Bhalla (1997)].

Proposition 6.1: *With fixed coefficient, a sufficient condition that trade liberalization raises aggregate employment is that urban employment increases, i.e., the M-sector is labour- intensive relative to the Y-sector.*

Proof :

Follows from the above discussion.

An interesting point to note is that such employment expansion is independent of the intensity ranking of traded final goods contrary to conventional wisdom. The flexible case is bit complicated. No longer are the LL′ and KK′ lines fixed. Consequent upon the tariff-induced change in factor prices, the variations in input coefficients shift these full employment constraints. Accordingly, the graphical analysis of employment change becomes a bit cumbersome. Beladi and Marjit (1996) have worked out the algebra in detail. Their conclusion is that with sufficiently small elasticity of substitution in agriculture, the result does not change qualitatively. Interestingly, if this elasticity is zero, the employment expansion is more pronounced with positive elasticity of factor substitution in Y and M sectors.

6.3.2 Foreign Capital Inflow

To analyze the employment effect of foreign capital inflow, we modify the above framework a little bit following Marjit, Broll and Mitra (1997). Suppose the intermediate good, now assumed to be traded and hence its price given from outside, is used in the production of the urban manufacturing good (Y) instead of the agricultural export good (X). Moreover, assume that the output and input tiers use different types of capital, K_I and K_M respectively. There are two types of foreign capital as well and as implicitly assumed earlier, foreign and domestic capitals of each type are perfect substitutes.

Suppose foreign capital flows in because of its domestic return being higher than the foreign return. To illustrate our case in the simplest possible manner, we assume that the inflow of foreign capital, of either type, that is allowed by the host-country government is small enough to warrant changes in the stock of capital and production in the rest of the world. On the other hand, the host-country is also assumed to be small enough so that changes in production therein, consequent upon such an inflow of foreign capital, does not affect the world prices either. Note that due to the assumption of the intermediate good being traded, the one-to-one correspondence between commodity and factor prices holds in the host-country under consideration, even with sector specific capital. Due to such independence of factor prices from factor endowments and any changes therein, caused by inflow of foreign capital, the rate of return to capital in the host-country does not change and get equalized with the world rate. On the other hand, by the above assumption of restricted inflow, despite of such persistence of difference in the rates of return to capital, foreign capital inflow is not significant enough to bring changes in production abroad and consequently in world prices which in turn can affect the factor prices. It is the employment of effect of such a small and restricted capital inflow that we are interested with. Of course, one can think of more general scenarios where capital inflow is unrestricted and perfect that brings down the rate of return to capital in the host country to the world rate. But the essence of the argument can still be captured in this simple thought experiment. What this essentially rules out is the factor substitution effects consequent upon changes in factor prices. Thus to analyze all we need is to examine how output levels change following such an inflow of foreign capital. The capital constraint is still binding unlike the case where capital inflow is unrestricted and the host-country is small enough to draw any amount of capital it likes from the world market without affecting its price. However, even if capital inflow that we consider here is small, it relaxes the constraint on production and enables greater utilization of other resources through production expansion. In essence it works in the same way as an accumulation of domestic capital in a small open economy.

How does the production pattern change due to such a capital inflow? Interestingly, only the change in agricultural production is relevant in this context. This is evident from the migration equation (6.6a) which, given (6.5), expresses aggregate employment as a function of wages and agricultural output:

$$L_e = \frac{W}{\bar{W}}\bar{L} + \left(1 - \frac{W}{\bar{W}}\right)a_{LX}X \tag{6.5a}$$

Thus, the only source of the expansionary effect of foreign capital inflow is the expansion of agricultural production. This sets the stage for our thought experiment.

Since the output tier now displays standard HOS properties --- output levels of X and Y being determined by availability of labour and K_1-type capital --- and domestic and foreign capitals are assumed to be perfect substitutes, a foreign capital inflow increases the stock of K_1 that reduces agricultural output through the standard output-magnification effect as long as the trade pattern is HO, i.e., the agricultural good is relatively labour-intensive[26]. Therefore, aggregate employment unambiguously falls.

What happens if K_M-type of foreign capital flows in? Such an inflow raises the production of the intermediate good which in turn makes less unskilled labour available for the output tier. Once again through the output-magnification effect

---

[26] Note that since the intermediate good M is now assumed to be traded, the output of Y is not constrained by its domestic production and hence by the availability of the sector-specific capital K_M.

the agricultural sector contracts if it is relatively labour intensive and through it the aggregate employment falls . Thus we have a rather strong result :

Proposition 6.2: *In an open economy Harris-Todaro model, regardless of the destination of the foreign investment, aggregate employment falls as long as the trade pattern is HO.*

The physical system of the HT model essentially displays the output-magnification effect just like the HOS model which guarantees the contractionary effect of a foreign capital inflow if export good is relatively labour intensive. With the rural wage tied down by the given commodity prices, aggregate employment varies directly with the output of the export good X [see (6.5a)]. But inflow of foreign capital lowers this output through the output magnification effect if it is relatively labour-intensive. Similar result holds in a typical HOS model if modified properly to sustain an initial unemployment-equilibrium without sacrificing the one-to-one correspondence between commodity and factor prices. The essence is that to raise aggregate employment, the production of relatively labour-intensive commodity must expand.

For a large capital inflow, on the other hand, that equalizes the domestic rate of return to capital with the world rate, we have an adverse factor substitution effect. This reinforces the contractionary effect.

6.4 General Equilibrium Analyses of Unemployment

There are essentially two types of unemployment analysis in a typical two-sector general equilibrium (GE) framework. In Brecher (1974) unemployment exists because of the downward rigidity of real wage prohibiting it to fall to a level required for maintaining full employment. Though this case of factor market distortion is to be distinguished from the case of wage-differential as in Bhagwati and Ramaswami (1963) and discussions of factor market distortions by Haberler (1950) and Johnson (1965), all of them belong to the same class in essence.

An alternative GE analysis of unemployment assumes downward rigidity of the money wage. However, as noted by Johnson (1965), when the wage is rigid in money terms rather than in real terms, in a typical HOS framework, it need not lead to unemployment per se. There are two ways in which one can modify the standard HOS model and talk about unemployment in presence of money wage rigidity. The first is to consider the three-factor or specific-factor variant of the HOS model. This enables us to study the link between money wage rigidity and unemployment directly. The other way is to consider production of a non-traded good. The non-traded model, often known as the Australian or dependent-economy model, has been used extensively in different contexts by Acharyya and Marjit (1998), Beladi and Marjit (1999), Helpman (1976), Jones and Corden (1976), Salter (1959) and Swan (1960). The existence of a non-traded good (like hair-cuts, housing) is the key element in explaining unemployment in a GE model and this fits well with the developing-country production structures. Accordingly, we shall often have recourse to this type of model in subsequent chapters. However, it is instructive to study in brief the other channels as well through which one can explain unemployment in a GE model. We begin with the discussion of real-wage rigidity following Brecher (1974) and then will move on to different cases of money-wage rigidity.

6.4.1 Minimum Real Wage

Consider the 2x2 HOS model discussed earlier. Under the standard assumptions and with wage flexibility, the full-employment output locus or the PPC would have been the smooth bowed-out curve AB in Figure 6.3. Suppose good Y is relatively labour intensive and the real wage is fixed at the level defined by the marginal productivity of labour in this sector at point E_o on AB. The corresponding commodity price ratio is denoted by p_o. Now an appeal to the Rybczynski theorem (or output-magnification effect) helps us trace out the PPC given this commodity price ratio and the corresponding fixed real wage as AE_oCB. The linear segment E_oC is the Rybczynski line. This traces out the fall in output of the labour-intensive good Y and corresponding increase in the relatively capital-intensive good X as labour endowment or employment falls given p_o. The broken bowed-out curves are PPCs corresponding to different employment levels that are tangent with the price line at corresponding points on this Rybczynski line. This indicates that all points on this line are efficient output combinations for different employment levels. Note that, except for point C, we have incomplete specialization together with unemployment, and as we go down this linear segment, unemployment increases.

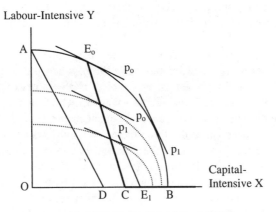

Figure 6.3: PPC Under Rigid Real Wage

The other segments of this PPC, AE_o and CB, are fundamentally different. Whereas along the latter we have unemployment with complete specialization in good X, any point along the former (except point A) indicates full employment with incomplete specialization. These are explained as follows.

For a smaller relative price of good Y, such as p_1 , by the Stolper-Samuelson theorem the real wage must fall below the level corresponding to p_o. But since downward rigidity of the real wage prevents this from actually falling to such a level, incomplete specialization is now unprofitable. The economy must now be completely specialized in the good X that requires less labour per unit of output. Such efficient output level will be at a point like E_1 But we still have unemployment. For prices even smaller leads us towards point B --- the full employment point. For prices higher than p_o, on the other hand, output equilibria occurs along the AE_o segment. This is because with the upward flexibility of the real wage, we have the standard output adjustments with full employment.

What appears from the above argument and Figure 6.3 is that whether full employment with incomplete specialization can be maintained for some relative commodity price (such as along AE_o) or not, depends on the level at which the real wage is downward rigid. For example, if the real wage is downward rigid at the level defined by the marginal physical product of labour in sector-Y at point A, the PPC becomes ADB with AD being the Rybczynski line so that except for the complete specialization points A and B, we always have unemployment. For simplicity, we confine ourselves with this case.

The next step is to translate such a PPC into an offer curve. Following the standard Marshallian procedure, this emerges to be the one labeled as $U_1A_1A_2U_2$ in Figure 6.4. The property of this offer curve is as follows. The kinks at points A_2 and A_1 correspond to full-employment, complete specialization points A and B in Figure 6.3. The movement from A_2 and A_1 along the linear segment corresponds to movement along the AD segment of the PPC towards point D and thus indicates successively lower employment. On the other hand, the movement along A_2U_2 towards U_2 implies constant employment at A whereas that along U_1A_1 towards U_1 implies successively higher level of employment (with corresponding movement being along DB towards B).

We are now in a position to analyze the employment implications of trade liberalization. Suppose initially there was a very high level of tariff that prohibited any trade between this home country and the foreign country. So the initial equilibrium was at the origin O. Note that by convention we have measured home exports (of labour-intensive good Y) along the horizontal axis. Assume that there is no minimum real wage restriction in foreign country so that it operates on the usual bowed-out full-employment PPC under standard assumptions of increasing opportunity cost resulting in non-linear offer curve throughout. When free trade is allowed, the equilibrium occurs at point E in Figure 6.4 where the foreign offer curve OF cuts the home offer curve. Clearly employment at home increases following trade liberalization. The reason is simple. Trade liberalization lowers output of home importables, good X in this example, and pushes the equilibrium in Figure 6.3 along AD towards point A thereby raising aggregate employment.

Of course, this expansionary effect of trade liberalization depends on the assumption that the country exports its relatively labour-intensive good Y:

Proposition 6.3 [Brecher (1974)]: *In a typical two-sector GE model of trade with minimum real wage restriction, trade liberalization raises aggregate employment if the trade pattern is HO.*

6.4.2 Money Wage Rigidity

Consider now the case where wage is frozen in money terms rather than in real terms. Moreover, instead of minimum wage, we assume that the money wage is fixed at some arbitrary level. As noted earlier, in two ways we can talk about the unemployment-equilibrium. We begin with the specific-factor model.

6.4.2.1 Unemployment in Specific-Factor Model

Consider the specific-factor model described in Chapter 4. But with homogeneous labour, we now assume that the two goods X and Y are produced by sector specific capital K_X and K_Y respectively in combination with sectorally mobile labour. Suppose good Y is imported and there is an initial ad-valorem tariff at the rate t. With the money wage now fixed (instead of just being rigid downward), given the ad-valorem tariff, the rates of return to the sector-specific capitals, r_X and r_Y, are determined uniquely by the world commodity prices:

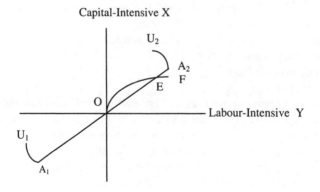

Figure 6.4: Trade and Unemployment Under
Downward Rigid Real Wage

$$P_X = a_{LX}\overline{W} + a_{KX}r_X \tag{6.11}$$

$$P_Y = a_{LY}\overline{W} + a_{KY}r_Y \tag{6.12}$$

where P_Y is the tariff-inclusive domestic price of good Y. Thus, as noted in Chapter 4, with the rigid money wage assumption even the specific factor model displays the HOS property : one-to-one correspondence between commodity and factor prices.

Since output levels are determined by the endowment of sector-specific capital and the value of the input-coefficient, if the money wage is fixed at a high level, unemployment will emerge.

The reason is simple. Suppose, given the commodity prices, (W^0, r_X^0, r_Y^0) is the set of factor prices for which all the factors were fully employed. This is shown in the Figure 6.5 as the point E through which the capital constraints (6.13) and (6.14) and the labour constraint pass. But if $\overline{W} > W^0$, as evident from the zero-profit conditions, the rates of return to capital must fall below r_X^0 and r_Y^0. Producers in both sectors then substitute cheaper capital for dearer labour. Consequently with $a_{Kj}(\overline{W}, r_j') > a_{Kj}(W^0, r_j^0)$ the capital constraints shift in whereas the labour constraint shifts out as $a_{Lj}(\overline{W}, r_j') < a_{Lj}(W^0, r_j^0)$. Consequently the output levels consistent with full employment of sector-specific capital stocks are no longer sufficient to ensure full employment labour. The corresponding level of employment is indicated by the line LeLe through point E_o. Given this as the initial position, how does trade liberalization affect aggregate employment? First of all, note that such a policy change lowers the domestic price of the import-competing good Y and consequently the rate of return to capital specific to this sector. Thus, due to the factor substitution effect, demand for labour and employment in this sector must fall. But the rate of return in the export sector does not change. So employment there remains constant. Therefore, aggregate employment unambiguously falls when trade is liberalized. Formally,

$$\hat{L}_e = \sigma_Y \lambda_{LY} \theta_{KY} \hat{P}_Y \tag{6.13}$$

where σ_Y is the elasticity of factor substitution in sector-Y.

In Figure 6.5 the K_Y-constraint shifts down resulting in a new equilibrium at a point like E_1 along the K_X-constraint indicating greater unemployment.

Inflow of foreign capital is, however, expansionary. This is regardless of the destination of foreign investment. As long as foreign and domestic capital are perfect substitutes, with factor prices and consequently input-coefficients tied to the given set of commodity prices, inflow of foreign capital raises output levels by relaxing the capital constraints. This in turn raises aggregate employment. Thus,

Proposition 6.4: *In a specific-factor model with rigid money wage, a) trade liberalization unambiguously lowers aggregate employment, b) a small inflow of foreign capital, regardless of its destination and type, generates   more employment.*

If capital inflow is large enough to depress the rate of return to capital, we have an adverse factor substitution effect on employment. Accordingly, the above result holds if factor-substitution elasticity is small.

Why is this result in striking contrast with the findings of Marjit, Beladi and Mitra (1997) discussed earlier? The difference is not due to the existence of intermediate good and/or the Harris-Todaro (HT) framework in their analysis. Rather, as mentioned earlier, employment change is determined there by the output magnification effect. But in the specific-factor model with rigid money wage, the standard output magnification does not work. Foreign capital raises the output of the sector where it flows in without reducing output of the other sector. Aggregate employment therefore increases unambiguously.

6.4.2.2 Dependent Economy Model

Consider a small dependent economy producing two goods : exportable, good X, and non-tradable, good N [27]. The export good is not domestically consumed. On the other hand, besides the non-traded good, the economy consumes a good Y that is entirely imported. We shall later relax this assumption of complete specialization.

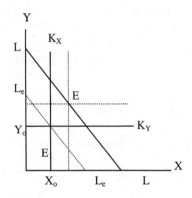

Figure 6.5: Unemployment in Specific-Factor Model

---

[27] The dependent economy model with or without imported input has been used to address a wide range of issues from the behaviour of the real exchange rate and trade surplus [Acharyya (1994a), Jones and Corden (1976), Salter (1959), Swan (1960)] to the employment effect of devaluation [Acharyya and Marjit (1998), Buffie (1984), Dornbusch (1980), Noman and Jones (1979), Helpman (1976) and Torvik (1994)].

By definition, the market for the non-traded good N must clear domestically:

$$D_N(p, y) = N \tag{6.14}$$

where $p \equiv P_N/P_M$ is the reciprocal of the real exchange rate for imports and y is the real income. This market-clearing condition, in fact, ensures that trade is balanced. Both the non-traded and the export goods are produced by domestic capital and labour. However, since domestic production of final imported good is not considered, to allow for tariff liberalization we assume that the export good uses an imported input (I) that is initially subjected to an ad-valorem tariff at the rate τ. This assumption is not at odds with reality. In India, for example, import intensity in export items like gems & jeweler, engineering goods and the like are still significantly high. To capture such high import intensity, we make the simplifying assumption that non-traded good does not require such an input. Given these assumptions, we write the zero-profit conditions as :

$$P_X = a_{LX}\overline{W} + a_{KX}r + (1+\tau)a_{IX}P_I^* \tag{6.15}$$

$$P_N = a_{LN}\overline{W} + a_{KN}r \tag{6.16}$$

Note that money wage rigidity makes price of the non-traded good independent of the domestic demand condition just like the traded good. Market-clearing condition (6.14) then indicates that domestic demand determines the output.

Once again the money wage set at a level higher than that consistent with full employment leads to an unemployment-equilibrium. Suppose production technology is Leontief, i.e., input coefficients are fixed. This assumption helps us understand the role of the non-traded good. Consider Figure 6.6 where point E represents the full-employment output combination. But for this to be the equilibrium, the full-employment supply of non-traded good must be demanded locally. Let (W^*, r^*) be the set of factor prices and p^* be the corresponding relative price of the non-traded good such that $D_N(p^*, y^*) = N^*$. Now if the money wage is set at a higher level, given the world price of export-good, the rate of return to capital must adjust downwards (falling below r^*) to make such production viable. Thus, labour-cost increases whereas the capital-cost falls in both the sectors. If the non-traded good is relatively labour-intensive, which is usually assumed because the non-traded sector mostly comprises of services, the non-traded price increases to p^o, say. For any given real income, this lowers the demand for non-traded good. Production must fall to adjust to this. Hence, the equilibrium must be somewhere along the EK$'$ segment of the capital constraint such as at point E_o. Unemployment emerges in the process. Note that this is independent of the assumption that non-tradable are relatively labour-intensive. If the non-traded good is capital-intensive, its price falls and output expands. Once again aggregate employment falls below the full-employment level.

The important point to note is that in the specific-factor model without any non-traded good, money wage pegged at a higher level led to unemployment by altering the input-coefficients. Had the input coefficients been fixed at the full employment levels, raising the money wage could in no way generate unemployment. But here even with fixed coefficients, unemployment emerges through fall (rise) in the demand for and hence output of the relatively labour (capital) intensive non-traded good.

In this framework it is straightforward to trace out the effect of trade liberalization. Lowering of tariff on imported input raises the rate of return to capital and hence the price of the non-traded good. Consequent fall in the demand for non-traded good lowers aggregate employment. But at the same time, since for this small open economy lowering of tariff means greater real income, demand for non-traded good and aggregate employment increase on this account. On balance, if the real income effect is not very strong, trade liberalization is contractionary.

How does an inflow of foreign capital affect aggregate employment? Once again it is unambiguously expansionary. Note that, with a rigid money wage, the rate of return to capital is linked to the world export price. Consequently, such an inflow of foreign capital only shifts the capital constraint in Figure 6.6 to the right without affecting demand for the non-traded good as long as it does not affect the world commodity prices. Therefore,

Proposition 6.5: *In a two-sector rigid wage dependent economy model, a) trade liberalization may be contractionary; b) foreign capital inflow is unambiguously expansionary for a given world prices.*

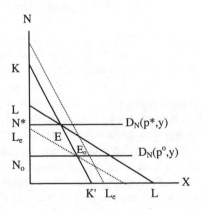

Figure 6.6: Output and Employment
          in a Dependent Economy

These results are very similar to those we can obtain in a specific-factor model. Do these results differ when domestic production of importables is considered? Of course not. Following example illustrates this. Suppose the non-traded good and an import-competing good (Y) use, in addition to labour hired at a fixed money wage, a particular type of capital, K_2, different from the capital used in export production, K_1. Returns to these two types of capital differ and are denoted by r_1 and r_2 respectively. The zero-profit conditions (6.15) and (6.16) are to be modified accordingly. The zero-profit condition for the production of the import-competing good is also subject to r_2. Thus, we now have a typical specific-factor structure as outlined above, with an additional sector producing a non-traded good. Aggregate employment now depends on the three output levels :

$$L_e = a_{LX}X + a_{LY}Y + a_{LN}N \tag{6.17}$$

If foreign capital flows only into the export sector that augments the stock of K_1-type of capital, export production increases. The non-traded price being demand-determined, and consequently the output of the import-competing good being determined by the net stock of K_2-type of capital, $K_2 - a_{LN}D_N(p, y)$, there would be no changes in these two output levels as long as the capital inflow is small enough as well as regulated in the sense defined above. Therefore, once again, under these circumstances, foreign capital inflow is expansionary.

By similar logic it should be clear that aggregate employment will increase if K_2-type of foreign capital flow in. But now such an expansion will be caused by an expansion of the import-competing production.

When the capital inflow is large enough to depress the domestic rate of return to capital to the world rate, world prices still need not change as long as the host-country is small. But now there will be factor substitution effect as well as a demand effect since the price of the non-traded good will be affected. To illustrate, consider a little modification of the production structure. Suppose, both the exportables and the import-competing good combine a third factor, say land (T), with labour and sector-specific capital. The reason for inclusion of such a factor will be clear shortly. Suppose, though land and capital can be substituted for each other, labour is used in fixed proportions in all these sectors. Essentially, by this assumption we rule out any substitution possibility between labour and other factors of production. This is, of course, a simplifying assumption.

With the rate of return to land, denoted by R, determined domestically, no longer factor prices are independent of the factor endowments. The three factor prices, (r_1, r_2, R), the price of the non-traded good and the three output levels are determined together by the three zero-profit conditions, the market-clearing condition for the non-traded good and the full employment conditions for the two types of capital and for land. The output levels then determine the level of employment.

Suppose the domestic rate of return to K_2-type of capital is higher than the world rate. This will attract this type of foreign capital from abroad and if such an inflow is unrestricted, the domestic rate will fall to the world level. The host-country being small, such inflow, however, will still have negligible impact on the stock of capital abroad. But, once the domestic rate of return to K_2-type of capital is linked to the world market, and is given to this small economy, we are back to the HOS world. More significantly, production of the import-competing good is no longer constrained by the domestic availability of this type of capital. Net availability of land, $T - a_{TX}X$, determines its production level. With world prices of traded goods unchanged, the drop in r_2 raises the return to land. This raises the cost of land in production of the export good and given its price and the money wage, the rate of return to K_1-type of capital should fall to make such production viable. Thus even though there is no inflow of K_1-type of foreign capital, its domestic return falls.

These changes in factor prices induce the producers to substitute land use by capital and the extent of such a substitution at the margin is determined by the elasticity of factor-substitution. But for a given stock of K_1-type of capital, such an intensive use of capital lowers export production. On this account employment falls. On the other hand, lower export production releases some of the land for production of the import-competing good. This enables such production to increase. Less intensive use of land there, in fact, magnifies such an expansion. This, in turn, raises the demand for labour. The drop in r_2 consequent upon inflow of K_2-type of foreign capital, on the other hand, lowers the supply price of the non-traded good and generates additional demand for it. Therefore, unless the contraction of export production is substantial, inflow of foreign capital is expansionary.

To summarize, foreign investment does appear to be expansionary in a dependent economy model regardless of whether domestic production of importable are allowed and whether the output or the input tier is the destination of such investment.

6.5   Employment and Welfare

Do employment changes have any implication for national welfare? It should, because this brings with it changes in labour income and consequently in national income. This was in fact discussed explicitly by Brecher (1974). At the outset, it seems more plausible that an employment expansion should imply higher welfare. But Brecher showed that welfare may paradoxically fall. This points out that the popular presumption about favourable impact of employment expansion on the level of welfare is not obvious. A curious little result has been obtained more recently by Beladi, Marjit and Frasca (1998). They demonstrate that in a HT framework, welfare changes depend *only* on the extent of trade distortion inspire of the existence of unemployment. The primary reason for this is that with rigid urban wage in a HT model, aggregate labour income does not *directly* depend on the level of employment. To see this, refer back to our discussion in section 6.3.2. Total labour income (I_L) equals,

$$I_L = Wa_{LX} X + \overline{W}(a_{LY}Y + a_{LM}M)$$
$$= W\overline{L} \tag{6.18}$$

Therefore, whether we have full employment or unemployment, and how the workforce is allocated across the sectors do not matter. Moreover, with the flexible rural wage determined from outside the economy, there is no indirect impact of changes in employment on labour income and welfare either. This result, Beladi et. al. point out is due to the envelope property that one gets even in a HT model with unemployment.

6.6 Conclusion

In this chapter we have discussed the employment effect of trade and investment liberalization that can be obtained in the standard trade models like the dual-economy and general equilibrium models. Trade liberalization appears to be expansionary when real wage is rigid downward. Otherwise, with money wage rigidity and no wage-differentials across sectors, employment falls in both specific-factor and dependent-economy frameworks. Of course, in all these cases, HO pattern of trade underlies the results.

Foreign investment, on the other hand is expansionary except in a HT dual-economy framework. More importantly, the destination of such foreign investment does not seem to matter much.

One might argue that since these models at best look at the formal-sector employment, the result that trade liberalization lowers aggregate employment, should not be taken too seriously. But a little reinterpretation of these results helps us understand that these models are not useless as they might appear to be. Even when the aggregate employment, taking formal and informal employment together, increases as is found to be the case in India, the contractionary effect of trade liberalization obtained above may be indicative of the fact that formal-sector employment has been substituted by informal-sector employment. Under such circumstances, the models do indicate impoverishment of the displaced formal-sector workforce. On the other hand, the fact that foreign capital inflow increases employment may indicate a reallocation of labour from the informal to the formal sector. By this we do not deny, of course, that these models are incomplete characterizations of the developing countries particularly as they do not incorporate segmented labour markets. But they set the stage for a more elaborate analysis of labour markets in the developing countries by indicating how labour is to be displaced from the formal sectors and pushed to the insecured informal markets through trade liberalization. In the subsequent chapters we address this issue more directly by appropriately extending some of the models discussed here.

IV

TRADE LIBERALIZATION, WAGE INEQUALITY AND EMPLOYMENT IN THE SOUTH

7 DIVERSE TRADE PATTERN, COMPLEMENTARITY AND FRAGMENTATION

7.1 Diverse Trade Pattern of Southern Countries

The major deficiency of the theories, used to explain wage movements in Southern countries, is a complete overlook of the diverse trade pattern reflected in the skill-intensity of their export items. Such diverse trade pattern cannot be effectively captured through an aggregative index of skill-intensity of exports. For example, India's export pattern alone reveals the drawback of such aggregate measures. From exporter of primary and agricultural products at large, India has emerged as a major exporter of software that is by any measure highly skill-intensive. Liberalization of investment and export opportunities has fuelled a boom in high-technology products that involve good deal of skilled labour. Thus, despite agricultural products being exported, it would not only be unfair but also perverse to assume India's exports as relatively unskilled-labour intensive while analyzing the terms of trade (TOT) and wage-gap nexus there. Quite a few East Asian and Latin American countries also have a wide range of skill-intensive exports.

Table 7.1 shows the structure of skill-intensive exports of Argentina, Brazil, China and India. Mayer and Wood (2000) classify diamond cut and pearls, chemicals, machinery and transport equipment (including computers) and scientific instruments as skill-intensive manufacturing exports whereas processed primary goods like non-ferrous metals as skill-intensive primary exports. On the other hand, high-technology exports, that include aerospace, computers, pharmaceuticals, scientific instruments and electrical machinery, are the skill-intensive goods according to Lall (2001). By both these criteria, the performances of these countries are quite impressive. Of course, the differences in the value of skill-intensive exports as a percentage of total exports in the two cases are due to the fact that the coverage of the former definition is much wider than that of the latter. Lall (2001) observes too that the increase in the developing country shares of high-technology and electronics exports in world exports have been quite phenomenal during 1985-1998. Almost one-fourth of world exports of high-technology goods and 35 percent of world exports of electronics now come from the developing countries.

Though, as spelled out earlier, trade volumes should not have any *direct* influence on factor prices as long as there are sufficiently large number of traded commodities ($m \geq n$), it may still be instructive to look at the numbers to judge the

Table 7.1
Skill-Intensive Exports of Selected Developing Countries

Skill-Intensive Items	Argentina			Brazil			China			India		
	1995	1997	1999	1995	1997	1999	1995	1997	1999	1995	1997	1998
I. Mayer and Wood's Definition												
1. Manufacture												
a. Chemicals (5)	14.338	15.769	16.488	14.997	16.482	12.182	10.145	9.311	10.998	14.164	12.108	11.046
b. Diamond cut, stones, etc. (667)	0.003	0.001	0.002	0.220	0.171	0.102	0.307	0.169	0.199	11.968	9.921	10.433
c. Machinery & Transport Equipment (7)	9.092	12.942	9.889	16.264	19.753	14.300	18.676	21.091	26.927	5.991	6.168	4.923
d. Scientific instruments (87-88)	2.292	2.578	2.581	2.943	3.192	2.077	2.401	1.966	2.383	1.939	1.871	1.966
2. Processed Primary												
e. Non-ferrous Metals (68)	1.173	0.887	0.894	3.406	2.747	1.883	1.149	1.234	1.257	0.401	0.575	0.282
Total (a - e) as % of Manufacturing Exports	26.898	32.176	29.853	37.830	42.345	30.544	32.678	33.772	41.764	34.462	30.643	28.650
II. Lall's Definition												
High Technology Exports As a % of Manufacturing Exports	4.097	5.128	7.658	5.198	7.751	13.399	10.466	13.137	17.209	5.806	6.550	5.621
As a % of Total Exports	1.161	1.502	2.000	2.361	3.594	4.336	7.790	9.891	13.553	3.408	3.744	2.981

Note: Numbers in the parentheses indicate SITC-2 commodity codes. Figures for categories a – e are all expressed as a percentage of manufacturing exports.

Source: UN Trade Commodity Statistics PC-TAS 2001; World Development Indicator 2001.

emerging diversified trade pattern for quite a good number of developing countries. Globalization and revolution in information technology have severely weakened the link between a country's abundant factors and its pattern of specialization. The conventional wisdom that the developing countries produce cheap textiles and agricultural exports because they are abundant in cheap labour and land, whereas rich countries produce more sophisticated products because they have the education and skill levels, has been put to test by the rapid growth of high-technology exports from the developing countries. Consequently, labeling the entire South as exporter of unskilled-labour intensive products and too much analytical dependence on the SS theorem, have often produced theoretical results that are largely at variance with the observed wage movements in the South.

But with a few exceptions [Marjit (1999), Marjit and Beladi (1998)] not much attention has been paid so far to the country-specific resource structure and diversified trade pattern while analyzing the widening wage-gap in the South. Every country is likely to produce and export goods whose resource requirements are consistent with its factor endowments, but this does not and should not mean that an unskilled-labour abundant country will export only the unskilled-labour intensive goods. Though even in a typical HOS model this can happen as pointed out in Chapter 4, the focus of the argument is on the trade pattern consistent with the product-specific factor endowments of a country. In case of India, for example, exports of rice and software are indeed consistent with the available product-specific resources. After all, factor-specificity of traded sectors in the developing countries is not an uncommon feature. Moreover, as pointed out by Robbins (1995a), there is some evidence of strong supply impact on wages in Latin America that also points towards traded goods using resources that are product-specific.

This chapter provides a class of simple structures that capture the diversified export pattern of the developing countries consistent with such product-specific factor endowments and reexamines the terms of trade-wage-gap nexus. The obvious way of modeling this type of diverse trade pattern beyond the symmetric HOS framework is to adopt a variant of the specific-factor model a la Jones (1971) described in Chapter 3. In such a framework, with two export goods varying in the skill-intensity, the strong result that we get is that irrespective of type of exports, an improvement in the terms of trade may lower the relative wage of the unskilled workers. Moreover, export-driven rise in price of the most unskilled-labour intensive agricultural product raises the money wage of the skilled labour that is not all used by agriculture. This happens because of the latent complementarity between skilled and unskilled exports. Thus for widening of the wage-gap it is not necessary that skill-intensive exports must grow or the terms of trade moves in its favour. As long as expansion of the unskilled-labour intensive exports affects the cost and production of the skill-intensive exports, wage-gap may widen. It is this complementarity which is typically absent in a two-good model. Such models infuse fresh outlook in explaining some of the apparently counter-intuitive empirical findings regarding distributional consequences of freer trade in many Southern countries. Apart from drawing heavily from Jones (1971), we also utilize a theoretical structure originally used by Gruen and Corden (1970) and later developed in Jones and Marjit (1992), Marjit (1990) and Marjit and Beladi (1996, 1999) and Findlay (1995). Two other issues addressed in terms of this type of a model are the employment implications of trade liberalization under alternative assumptions of wage rigidity and the effects of agricultural reforms on wage inequality.

Of late, several authors have analyzed the issue of fragmentation in world trade whereby different countries increasingly specialize in different fragments of production activities [Deardorff (1998), Harris (1993, 1995), Jones and Kierzkowski (2001a, b)]. Sharp decline in transportation and communication costs makes it possible for the production process to be fragmented and traded across the globe. It has now become much easier to specialize in parts rather than produce and export the finished final good. Products that might 10 years ago have been produced in a single country are now made up of components that have crossed dozens of borders before final assembly. International trade in *fragments*, thus is now the order of the day. Such intra-product trade or fragmented global production has also driven the rapid growth of exports from the developing countries. This means, fragmentation by itself can lead to an increase in wage inequality in a particular country. In Chapter 5 we discussed how trade in intermediate good in a typical HOS framework can explain symmetric wage-gap phenomenon. Here in section 7.3, drawing heavily from Marjit and Beladi (1998), we examine the distributional consequences of commodity price movements with or without fragmentation.

7.2 Complementarity and the Wage-Gap

7.2.1 A Simple Model with Diverse Trade Pattern

Consider a small open economy producing three goods : an agricultural good (X) that uses unskilled labour (L), land (T) and imported fertilizer (F); manufacturing good (Y) using unskilled labour and capital (K); and manufacturing good (Z) that uses skilled labour (S) and capital. To begin with, we assume that the country concerned exports Z and imports Y. Agricultural good X is the potential exportable. But initial trade restrictions prohibit farmers and traders to take advantage of the higher world price. Thus, initially, the country exports only the skill-intensive manufacturing good (Z). The domestic (pre-trade) price of agricultural good is, however, set by the local government. Moreover, we assume that the import of fertilizer used by agriculture is subsidized. The assumed initial situation is purpose specific. This allows us to focus on the implications of tying up the local farm price with the higher world price that are much talked about of late, particularly after the success of Vietnam as a major exporter of rice. Of course, we are not concerned here with the inherent long run problem of falling and fluctuating world prices for agricultural goods that an exporting country might face, as witnessed by, for example, the coffee producers of Africa and Latin-America [Oxfam (2002)]. Here we are concerned *only* with the short run distributional implications of liberalization of agriculture and of exports of agricultural goods for a *given* world price.

These above set of assumptions in regard to the agricultural production and pricing are, of course, not at odds with reality. In almost every part of the world, the developing as well as the developed, agriculture is protected in some form or the other. It has always been easier to get political support for such protection, from both the pro and anti globalization camps. As a result agricultural protection has persisted even in the era of globalization. This takes different forms including price supports and production subsidies to the farmers. In India, for example, the bulk of the marketable surplus of important crops like rice is procured by the government at the price set by the Agricultural Price Commission, usually at a higher level than the market-clearing one, and then part of it is distributed at a subsidized price to the poor through the public distribution systems and the rest is retained as buffer stocks for the bad harvest periods. Prices of pulses and sugar are similarly set. In the European Union countries, the prices of agricultural products are set at a common and artificially high level across the member countries under the Common Agricultural Policy established in the 1957 Rome Treaty, with a system of shared financial responsibility for guaranteeing prices. Surplus productions bought from the farmers are partly stored and the rest is dumped in the world market. On the other hand, agriculture is subsidized heavily not only in the developing countries but also in advanced industrialized countries of Europe, in Japan and in the US. Subsidies stand tall even during the present era of globalization. Throughout the 1990s, subsidies provided by the European and the US governments have in fact increased. This has now become a bone of contention for the trade negotiations between developing and developed countries.

With such an initial situation of no trade and administered price for agriculture, P_X, subsidy on the use of (imported) fertilizer and prices of the manufactured export and import-competing goods, P_Z and P_Y, being determined in the world market, the following competitive zero-profit conditions define the price system of this economy :

$$P_X = a_{LX}W + a_{TX}R + (1 - s)a_{FX}P_F \tag{7.1}$$

$$P_Y = a_{LY}W + a_{KY}\,r \tag{7.2}$$

$$P_Z = a_{SZ}W_S + a_{KZ}\,r \tag{7.3}$$

Of course, one should distinguish between the high procurement price and the subsidized price at which foodgrains are sold through the public distribution system in many countries. Since such selling price is usually set at a level lower than the market-clearing price and the agricultural production is fixed by the availability of land (see eq. (7.7) below), there will be an excess demand for agricultural good. Accordingly, either demand is rationed or such excess demand is met through initial stock of foodgrains. However, given our purpose, we make things simpler by assuming that the procurement and selling prices are the same and that such a price, P_X in (7.1), is set at the market-clearing level so that initially we need not bother about any excess demand for foodgrains.

We close the model by bringing in the conditions for full employment of all the factors ensured by flexibility in the factor prices :

$$\bar{S} = a_{SZ}Z \tag{7.4}$$

$$\bar{K} = a_{KY}Y + a_{KZ}Z \tag{7.5}$$

$$\bar{L} = a_{LX}X + a_{LY}Y \tag{7.6}$$

$$\bar{T} = a_{TX}X \tag{7.7}$$

This structure is, in fact, a composition of two specific-factor models. The general equilibrium solution of the model is fairly standard with the above set of seven independent equations determining seven variables.

7.2.2 Skill-Intensive Exports and the Wage-Gap

To analyze the trade and wage-gap nexus, first consider a case where booming global trade prospects increase the price of the skill-intensive good Z. It is obvious that such a price increase will raise the skilled wage and the return to capital and reduce the unskilled money wage, thereby increasing the wage-gap. The argument is simple. Let us consider a given value of agricultural output X and hence the amount of unskilled labour that produces it. Then (7.2) - (7.6) give us a typical specific-factor set up. An increase in P_Z then increases the rent for the skilled workers *specific* in this sector and the return to the *mobile* factor, capital. But the wage of the unskilled workers, specific in the Y-sector when the Y - Z nugget is considered, must fall. However, as the unskilled wage goes down, unskilled labour moves to agriculture halting such decline to some extent. But production of import-competing good Y must get reduced at the end as capital leaves for the skill-intensive export sector Z. In the new equilibrium the unskilled-wage must have fallen and the skilled-wage must have risen[28]. This just shows that the pattern of exports matters in the relative wage movement.

---

[28] For a very small increase in price of manufactured exports, we can neglect the consequent real income gains and the increased domestic demand for agriculture.

7.2.3 Agricultural Trade Liberalization and Complementarity

One of the agenda of the ongoing reform process in India is to free agricultural trade by tying up the agricultural price with the world price. Many of the agricultural products like wheat, poultry and dairy products, sugar, fruits and nuts, cost much less than the world prices. But until now trade restrictions did not allow the Indian farmers to take advantage of such higher world prices. It is only recently, the Government of India is encouraging agricultural exports, except a few commodities like jute, and for the purpose is providing the transport subsidy. Even if all agricultural subsidies are removed, there are a wide range of agricultural products that can be exported at a lower price, provided of course the industrial countries remove their subsidies too and provides the market access. Many South Asian countries have similar cost advantage. Under such circumstances, liberalizing agricultural trade should equalize the domestic (administered) price P_X with the higher world price if the country is small producer of agricultural goods and hence is a price taker in the world market. Otherwise, the domestic and world prices will be equalized at a level lower than the initial world price but certainly higher than the pre-liberalization domestic price. That is, in either case P_X increases as a consequence of agricultural trade liberalization.

With the increased demand for unskilled labour in the agricultural activity consequent upon such price increase, the unskilled-wage increases. The increased money wage-bill in the import competing sector Y, on the other hand, causes its production to contract and with it pushes down the rate of return to capital to maintain the zero-profit condition there. In the skill-intensive export sector the lower capital cost, in turn, encourages production and raises the wage of the scarce skilled labour. Therefore, both the unskilled and skilled wages increase making the change in wage-gap ambiguous following an increase in the price of agricultural exports. Formally,

$$\hat{W}_S - \hat{W} = -\left[\frac{\theta_{KZ} - \theta_{KY}}{\theta_{SZ}\theta_{LY}} \right]\hat{r} \tag{7.8}$$

What is to be noted is that agricultural trade liberalization raises the return to the skilled labour used only in the manufacturing export sector. This sector expands as well because as a consequence of the higher relative price of skilled labour, the producers choose relatively less skill-intensive technique which releases few skilled labour per unit of output and makes possible to use them in production of the additional output [see eq. (7.7)]. The required capital for such expansion of the manufacturing exports is drawn from the manufacturing import sector which contracts because unskilled workers migrate to agriculture where money wage had risen initially (see appendix). Therefore, expansion of agriculture induced by trade not only raises the return to the skilled workers in the manufacturing export sector but also leads to an expansion in its size. This latent complementarity between agricultural exports and skill-intensive manufacturing exports is an important feature of the developing countries with bimodal comparative advantage and is crucial for understanding the widening wage-gap.

As evident from (7.8), agricultural trade liberalization widens the wage-gap only if $\theta_{KZ} > \theta_{KY}$. This condition tells us that the savings on capital cost is more in the skill-intensive export sector than in the unskill-intensive import-competing sector. Hence the skilled-wage should increase more than the unskilled-wage thereby widening the wage-gap, notwithstanding the fact that it is the agriculture, that does not use skilled labour, has expanded. The latent complementarity between agriculture and the skilled manufacturing leads to growing wage inequality.

A drop in the rate of return to capital raises the skilled wage rate and this is crucial for a possible widening of the wage-gap. Of course, if capital is sectorally immobile or skill-intensive export require specific type of capital to work with the skilled labour, the skill money wage would not have increased. Hence, mobility or sector-specificity of capital assumes an important role in the whole exercise and connects the rise in price of agricultural good to an increase in the skilled-wage. Any empirical investigation regarding this must incorporate such effect explicitly. Intersectoral mobility of capital, as we show later, continues to be fairly important even in a more complex and realistic characterization of the labour markets. Therefore,

Proposition 7.1: Agricultural trade liberalization widens the wage-gap only if $\theta_{KZ} > \theta_{KY}$.

Proof :
Follows from the above discussion.

Note that as the agricultural output expands and since the endowment of land is given, the real unskilled-wage, W/P_X, must fall. This is the case where a rise in the price of unskilled-labour intensive exports leads to a decline in the real wage of the unskilled and widens the wage-gap. This result is consistent with the fact that the consumption basket of the unskilled is loaded in favour of food. It seems that if a country has comparative advantage in Y, the wage-gap must decline when its price falls. In a way this is interesting because even if $\theta_{LX} > \theta_{LY} > \theta_{LZ} = 0$, export-driven rise in the price of unskilled-labour intensive manufacturing (Y) reduces the wage inequality whereas increase in the price of unskilled-labour intensive agriculture may actually increase the wage inequality.

What would be the effect of capital inflow? Typically this will lower the rate of return to capital in the host country. In the new equilibrium it settles down to the international rate r^*. Given the prices of the skilled and unskilled manufactures, we determine the skilled and unskilled wages from zero-profit conditions in these sectors and then similar condition for the agriculture determines the rate of return to land. Clearly, with the rate of return to capital now lower, both the unskilled and skilled wages will increase. Once again, as argued earlier, the wage-gap will widen if $\theta_{KZ} > \theta_{KY}$.

7.2.4 Agricultural Subsidy and Income Distribution

Production subsidies have traditionally been one of the major policy instrument to protect agriculture in many countries. In India, subsidies on fertilizer and on the use of electricity for irrigation are the major ones that, as the skeptics argue, have mostly benefited the larger farmers. It has now been one of the main agenda of the WTO and its member countries to remove such subsidies. This has led to one of the heated policy debates in India. These reforms have far-reaching implications, some of which can only be analyzed meaningfully in a dynamic context. However, even remaining within the scope of the above static framework, we can discuss their effects on wage inequality. This has to do with the continuation of fertilizer subsidy for the farmers, big and small. The policy exercise is equivalent to the one where price of the fertilizer is effectively reduced for everyone. It is interesting to examine the implications of such subsidy reforms for different land-holding sizes.

One essential difference between large and small holding (or family farming) is the different production technologies used. It is for such differences, the effect of subsidy reform is expected to be different. To illustrate, assume that in the small holdings or family farming, the family members offer their own labour to cultivate the small piece of land that they own. To make things simple, suppose that all input coefficients are fixed. Now the typical scenario in agriculture in many developing countries is involvement of too many family members in relation to the relatively small piece of land. Given the assumption of fixed technology, this amounts to surplus workers. To set aside the issue of underemployment till the last chapter, suppose these surplus workers work in the large holding at the money wage prevailing in the market. Given full mobility, this means that return to those who work in family farming must be equal to such wage rate. Under these circumstances, with very low land-labour ratio in the family farming, a rise in the money wage following subsidy reduction may imply larger income for the family even though return to land falls.

Suppose the underlying production function for agriculture permits only two types of technique of production expressed in terms of the corresponding input coefficients : $\tilde{a}_{iX}$ and a_{iX}, $i = L, T, F$. Let $\tilde{a}_{iX}$ and a_{iX} be the input coefficients in family farming and in large holdings respectively. The following restrictions on these coefficients capture the difference in large and small holdings :

$$\tilde{a}_{LX} > a_{LX}, \tilde{a}_{TX} < a_{TX}, \tilde{a}_{FX} < a_{FX} \tag{7.9}$$

With the two zero-profit conditions written in terms of the effective prices, given the world prices of agriculture and fertilizer,

$$P_X - (1-s)a_{FX}P_F^* = a_{LX}W + a_{TX}R \tag{7.10}$$

$$P_X - (1-s)\tilde{a}_{FX}P_F^* = \tilde{a}_{LX}W + \tilde{a}_{TX}R \tag{7.11}$$

it is immediate that, given (7.9), the effect of reduction in fertilizer subsidy is essentially the Stolper-Samuelson result: With the effective price of agricultural output of the large holding falling more than that of the small holding, the return to land that is used intensively relative to labour there falls (more than proportionately) whereas the money wage may increase (if so, once again, more than proportionately). Therefore, subsidy reform may in fact benefit small holdings. This result is in fact similar to what we find even in rich developed countries with historically higher levels of agricultural protection and subsidization. There has been overwhelming evidence that the main beneficiaries of farm support in the EU and the US are the largest farmers [Oxfam (2002)].

7.3 Liberalization and Employment

It is interesting to see how the diversified trade pattern and the complementarity between export sectors alter the trade and employment nexus discussed in Chapter 6. For analytical exposition once again we consider unemployment of unskilled labour only.

As is evident from the discussions in Chapter 6, some kind of wage rigidity must be there that prohibits unskilled labour to be fully employed. In the following we begin with the money-wage rigidity.

7.3.1   Money-Wage Rigidity

Once the money wage is fixed at some level $\overline{W}$, the model specified in (7.1) - (7.7) displays the HOS property: Factor prices are uniquely determined by the given world commodity prices. Clearly, for such a wage rate fixed at a level higher than the full employment level, the return to both capital and land fall below the corresponding full-employment levels whereas the skilled-wage goes up. The induced factor-substitution effects in the export sectors then raise the production of skilled export good,

$$\hat{Z} = -\hat{a}_{SZ} \tag{7.12}$$

and lowers production of agricultural export,

$$\hat{X} = -\hat{a}_{TX} \tag{7.13}$$

Since domestic capital was already fully employed and agricultural export production does not require capital, expansion of the manufacturing export production can be sustained only through the contraction of the import-competing production and consequent release of capital. With production of both import-competing good and agricultural good falling, and producers switching to relatively less labour-intensive techniques in these sectors, aggregate employment of unskilled labour must fall below the full employment level.

Given such an initial unemployment, does trade liberalization reduce or raise it further? Not surprisingly, unemployment increases. A tariff cut lowers domestic price and production of the import-competing good. Production adjustment causes both the unskilled labour and capital to be displaced at initial technique of production. On the other hand, with the unskilled money wage pegged, the burden of downward adjustment in the price is borne entirely by the domestic capital through a fall in its return. This causes producers in both the Z and Y sectors to use relatively more capital-intensive techniques. With less skilled-labour intensive technique being chosen, production of export good-Z increases too [see (7.4)]. All these make room for the released capital from the contracting Y-sector to be absorbed fully. At the same time, a few unskilled labour is displaced further from the import-competing sector reinforcing the initial contraction in industrial employment.

But given the rigid money wage, and import-tariff reduction not affecting the world price of the agricultural export (due to the small country assumption), the rate of return to land (R) remains unchanged. Thus, neither there will be any factor-substitution effect nor any output effect in agriculture and consequently there should not be any change in the agricultural employment. On the whole, aggregate employment unambiguously falls. Algebraically,

$$\hat{L}_e = \sigma_X \lambda_{LX} \hat{R} + \lambda_{LY}(\hat{a}_{LY} + \hat{Y}) \tag{7.14}$$

The first term on the right hand side captures the change in agricultural employment through the factor-substitution effect whereas the second term captures the change in industrial employment through both the factor-substitution and output effects. Since $\hat{R} = 0$ and both $\hat{a}_{LY}$ and $\hat{Y}$ are negative so aggregate employment falls through a contraction of the industrial employment in the import-competing sector with no accommodating change in agricultural employment.

Agricultural trade liberalization that raises the domestic price is also expansionary. But now the industrial employment remains unchanged because rate of return to capital and the skilled money wage are not affected. Only the return to land increases that induces the farmers to use labour more intensively to the extent permissible by the technology. Thus agricultural employment expands through the factor substitution effect.

7.3.2 Real-Wage Rigidity

Suppose now that the unskilled-wage is fixed in real terms instead of in money terms. Assuming that the skilled labour intensive export good is not consumed by the unskilled working population, following wage indexation is reasonable :

$$\hat{W} = \alpha \hat{P}_X + (1-\alpha)\hat{P}_Y \tag{7.15}$$

where α is the (constant) share of expenditure by the unskilled workers on the agricultural good. If $\alpha = 1$, the real wage is fixed in terms of the agricultural good.

With the flexibility of money wage to the extent defined in (7.15), import liberalization will now affect agricultural employment. In particular, as shown in the appendix,

$$\hat{L}_e = \left[-\sigma_X \lambda_{LX} \frac{\theta_{LX}}{\theta_{TX}}(1-\alpha) + \lambda_{LY} \left\{ \frac{\alpha\sigma_Y}{\theta_{KY}} + \frac{\sigma_Z\lambda_{KZ}}{\lambda_{KY}\theta_{SZ}}(1-(1-\alpha)\theta_{LY}) \right\} \right] \hat{P}_Y \tag{7.16}$$

Once again the first term in the parenthesis indicates the change in agricultural employment and since $\hat{P}_Y < 0$, this is positive. Thus, though industrial employment falls as before, agricultural employment now increases. Consequently, the aggregate employment falls only if σ_X, the factor-substitution elasticity in agriculture, is small or the real wage is fixed in terms of the agricultural good only. In the latter case, this boils down to money wage rigidity in essence and the employment effect is identical to the previous case.

7.4 Fragmentation and the Wage-Gap

The issue of international fragmentation of production processes and the resultant changes in factor allocation and prices in the local market has come up for discussion in several recent papers by Jones (2001), Jones and Kierzkowski (2001b) and Jones and Marjit (2001a). Suppose in addition to the three final goods, the small open economy also produces a local variety of an intermediate good (M) that is used in the skilled manufacturing export sector instead of capital. This intermediate good is produced by skilled labour and capital. The zero-profit condition (7.3) for the skilled manufacturing exports should now be rewritten as :

$$P_Z = a_{SZ}W_S + a_{mZ}P_m \tag{7.17}$$

where P_m is the (domestic) price of the local variety of the intermediate good :

$$P_m = a_{Sm}W_S + a_{Km}r \tag{7.18}$$

Full employment conditions for skilled labour and domestic capital should also be changed accordingly.

To start with the intermediate good is produced within the economy because the possibility of accessing the lower priced intermediate from abroad is impeded by fixed costs of transportation and communication. For example, certain services can be used only via internet facilities. Without the possibility of using the on-line facility, certain local resources need to be spent which may be quite expensive. Satellite communications may entail fixed costs (F) and that will be the basic problem of accessing the intermediate good from abroad. In particular, we assume such foreign input is cheaper :

$$P_m^* < P_m \qquad (7.19)$$

It is obvious that given the price of the skilled manufacturing export good, a fall in price of the local variety of the input will raise the skilled-wage. Let W_S^* be the corresponding skilled-wage when the price of the input is P_m^*. Thus, if $(W_S^* - W_S)S < F$, producers or skilled entrepreneurs do not have any incentive for using the foreign intermediate good. Figure 7.1 captures the incentive for fragmentation, i.e., accessing the cheaper intermediate good from abroad. Note that for $P_m^* \in [\overline{P}_m^*, P_m]$, lower priced intermediate will not be used. It is assumed that the skilled labour sector as a whole decide on using the better intermediate good and decide on incurring the fixed cost, and if $P_m^* < \overline{P}_m^*$ only then import takes place. It is straightforward to argue that a lower F and/or higher S will increase $\overline{P}_m^*$, the critical minimum price of the foreign intermediate for which the local users will go for the foreign input. Suppose a decline in F now makes it possible for the producers to pay P_m^* and this is what we define as fragmentation in our framework.

However, lowering of the price of the intermediate good to P_m^* has immediate impact on factor prices. Both the skilled and unskilled wages go up whereas the rate of return to capital falls. Therefore,

Proposition 7.2 : *Fragmentation will imply a decline (an increase) in the wage-gap provided skilled manufacturing export sector is less (more) capital intensive relative to the importable good.*

Proof :

Simple algebraic manipulations yield,

$$\hat{W}_S - \hat{W} > 0 \quad \text{only if} \quad \left[\tilde{\theta}_{SX}\theta_{KY} - \theta_{Km}\theta_{mX}\theta_{LY}\right]\hat{P}_m > 0 \qquad (7.20)$$

where, $\tilde{\theta}_{SX} = \theta_{SX} + \theta_{Sm}\theta_{mX}$.

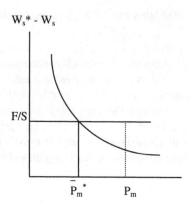

Figure 7.1: Fragmentation

If $\hat{P}_m < 0$, due to the possibility of fragmentation, the wage-gap will go up if skilled manufacturing export good is capital intensive relative to manufacturing imports. One interpretation of this result is that with a lower rate of return to capital following fragmentation, both the skilled and unskilled workers gain in terms of their money wages. Once again, if the skilled manufacturing sector uses capital more intensively than the unskilled manufacturing sector, it saves capital costs to a greater extent allowing the skilled-wage to rise more than the unskilled-wage and consequently the wage-gap increases. What is to be noted is that in case of the unskilled manufacturing sector, the measure of intensities is in terms of direct requirement of capital, whereas for the skilled manufacturing export sector capital requirement is measured indirectly through the production of the intermediate good.

7.5 Terms of Trade, Fragmentation and Wage Inequality

We have so far discussed the distributional implications of fragmentation whereby a drop in the fixed cost (F) converts the intermediate good into a traded input, i.e., induces producers to access the foreign intermediate good. What distributional consequences we can expect of the change in the terms of trade in presence of fragmentation?

Consider first the case of agricultural trade liberalization. With the administered agricultural price now tied up with the higher world price, producers are encouraged to expand agricultural output necessitating more unskilled labour. But with the initial full employment additional labour can be obtained only from the import-competing manufacturing sector Y through fall in its production. This process drives up the unskilled wage and must reduce the return to capital since capital is now in excess following the contraction of the Y-sector. The lower capital cost makes the local variety of the intermediate good cheaper and the corresponding lower input cost in skilled-manufacturing export sector, given its world price, benefits the skilled worker. With $\hat{r} < 0$, it is straightforward to check that the wage-gap widens only if (7.20) holds.

Now consider the case of fragmentation, i.e., where the intermediate good can be bought and sold in the international market at a price P_m^*. It is then straightforward to check that an increase in world price of agriculture only reduces the return to land without affecting either the skilled or the unskilled wage. The wage-gap, therefore, remains unchanged. What is really surprising to note is that the unskilled workers do not benefit from such price increase. Rather, their real wage goes down.

What are the effects of an increase in world price of the skilled-manufacturing exports (Z)? At initial output and employment levels in agriculture, such price increase raises skilled-wage and reduces the unskilled-wage in the rest of the economy. This is because the production structure of the rest of the economy, defined by (7.2), (7.17) and (7.18), resembles the specific-factor model with skilled and unskilled labour as the two immobile factors and capital as the mobile factor. This is immediate once we substitute (7.18) in (7.17). The falling wage induces unskilled workers to move to agriculture reducing wages there as well. With lower labour costs, agricultural activity gets a boost but scarcity of land only causes an increase in its return. All these developments arrest the fall in unskilled-wage to some extent but cannot reverse the direction of change because in the final equilibrium the increase in return to land necessitates a lower wage to maintain zero-profit condition given the world price of agricultural exports. At the end, the wage-gap widens.

With fragmentation, however, things become less certain. As explained earlier, fragmentation raises the skilled-wage and reduces the rate of return to capital. But lower capital cost encourages the production of the import-competing good. The consequent increase in demand for unskilled labour raises its wage too. Once again the factor intensities become important. In particular, the wage-gap widens only if the import-competing sector is capital intensive relative to the sector producing the intermediate good.

7.6 Conclusion

Export of agriculture and diversified manufacturing are key features of many developing countries in Asia and Latin-America. Complementarity between different export goods can be an important factor in the explanation of widening wage-gap in Southern countries. Because of this complementarity, increase in price of agricultural exports that uses unskilled labour more intensively may paradoxically tilt the income distribution in favour of the skilled workforce employed elsewhere. For similar reasons capital inflow in such an economy may widen the wage-gap.

Fragmentation is another channel through which the wage-gap may widen. Not only fragmentation per se is important, it also influences the terms of trade improvement and the wage-gap relationship significantly.

With rigidity of unskilled money wage, trade and investment liberalization have employment implications as well. Once again focusing on the organized-sector employment as in Chapter 6, we observe that when the unskilled-wage is rigid in money terms, trade liberalization is unambiguously contractionary. This is similar to the result we got in a specific-factor model though the channels through which the effects work in the two cases are quite different. Interestingly, trade liberalization reduces industrial employment leaving agricultural employment unchanged. Since in the LDCs, agriculture is predominantly an informal sector, this result has far reaching implication as we shall spell out in the next Chapter. But when the unskilled-wage is rigid in real terms, contractionary effect follows only when factor-substitution elasticity in agriculture is very low.

APPENDIX

I. Agricultural Trade Liberalization

From the full employment conditions for capital and skilled labour we get,

$$\hat{K} = 0 = \lambda_{KY}(\hat{a}_{KY} + \hat{Y}) + \lambda_{KZ}(\hat{a}_{KZ} + \hat{Z}) \tag{A.7.1}$$

$$\hat{S} = 0 = \hat{a}_{SZ} + \hat{Z} \tag{A.7.2}$$

Given $\sigma_Z = (\hat{a}_{KZ} - \hat{a}_{SZ})/(\hat{W}_S - \hat{r})$, these two yield the change in production of the import-competing good:

$$\hat{Y} = -\hat{a}_{KY} + \sigma_Z \frac{\lambda_{KZ}}{\lambda_{KY}\theta_{SZ}} \hat{r} \tag{A.7.3}$$

On the other hand, using (A.7.3) and definitions of σ_X and σ_Y, from the full employment condition for labour we can derive the following:

$$\hat{L} = 0 = -\sigma_X \lambda_{LX}(\hat{W} - \hat{R}) + \left[\sigma_Y \frac{\lambda_{LY}}{\theta_{LY}} + \sigma_Z \frac{\lambda_{KZ}\lambda_{LY}}{\lambda_{KY}\theta_{SZ}}\right]\hat{r}$$

By $\hat{P}_X = \theta_{LX}\hat{W} + \theta_{TX}\hat{R}$ and $\hat{P}_Y = 0 = \theta_{LY}\hat{W} + \theta_{KY}\hat{r}$, this boils down to,

$$\hat{r} = \frac{-\sigma_X \frac{\lambda_{LX}}{\theta_{TX}}}{\left[\sigma_X \frac{\lambda_{LX}\theta_{KY}}{\theta_{LY}\theta_{TX}} + \sigma_Y \frac{\lambda_{LY}}{\theta_{LY}} + \sigma_Z \frac{\lambda_{KZ}\lambda_{LY}}{\lambda_{KY}\theta_{SZ}}\right]} \hat{P}_X < 0 \qquad (A.7.4)$$

Refering back to (A.7.3), it is now immediate that as $\hat{r} < 0$, so $\hat{a}_{KY} < 0$, and hence the production of the import-competing good falls.

II. Change in Employment Under Real-Wage Rigidity

Using (7.15), and given $\hat{P}_X > 0 = \hat{P}_Y = \hat{P}_Z$ through agricultural trade liberalization, the change in rate of return to capital can be obtained from (7.2) in the text :

$$\hat{r} = \frac{[1 - (1-\alpha)\theta_{LY}]}{\theta_{KY}} \hat{P}_Y \qquad (A.7.5)$$

Similarly from (7.1) we get the change in return to land as :

$$\hat{R} = (1-\alpha)\frac{\theta_{LX}}{\theta_{TX}} \hat{P}_Y \qquad (A.7.6)$$

Hence,

$$\hat{W} - \hat{r} = -\frac{\alpha}{\theta_{KY}} \hat{P}_Y$$

Finally, recalling the change in employment from (7.14) in the text, and using

$$\hat{Y} = -\hat{a}_{KY} + \sigma_Z \frac{\lambda_{KZ}}{\lambda_{KY}\theta_{SZ}}$$

and the above expressions for factor price changes, we obtain :

$$\hat{L}_e = \alpha_X \lambda_{LX} \hat{R} + \lambda_{LY}(\hat{a}_{LY} + \hat{Y})$$

$$= \alpha_X \lambda_{LX} \hat{R} + \lambda_{LY}(\hat{a}_{LY} - \hat{a}_{KY} + \sigma_Z \frac{\lambda_{KZ}}{\lambda_{KY}\theta_{SZ}} \hat{r})$$

Hence by (A.7.5) and the definition of factor substitution elasticity in sector-Z (σ_Z), this boils down to (7.16) in the text.

8 SEGMENTED INPUT MARKETS AND NON-TRADED GOOD

8.1 Segmented Labour Markets in the South

Labour markets in LDCs are usually segmented into formal (or organized) and informal (or unorganized) sectors. Typically the formal sector is the high-wage, unionized sector with job security and fringe benefits whereas in the informal or unorganized sectors, wages are determined by market forces, are low compared to the unionized sectors and jobs are mostly casual. Self-employed petty producers and traders in the informal sectors are often those who cannot get jobs in the high-wage organized segment of the labour market. As well documented in Agenor (1996), Cole and Sanders (1985), Fields (1990) and Mazumdar (1983, 1993), about sixty percent of total labour force in the developing world are employed in such non-unionized informal sectors. In case of India, according to the 1991 Census Report, the figure is staggering ninety percent during the 1980s. The situation has not changed much in the 1990s. In fact, Dev (2000) finds that during 1973-1993, in almost all the sectors the share of informal segments has either remained the same or has increased. This has been highest in agriculture around 99 percent, followed by about 90 and 81 percents respectively in construction and manufacturing.

Typically LDCs have an employment growth rate in the formal sectors well below the growth rate of the workforce. As pointed out by Mazumdar (1983), in some situations the "increase in the least cost efficiency wage of labour with technological progress is central to this development". In some cases, the public sector, being a large employer besides agriculture, has contributed to this by yielding to pressures to increase wages that reduces its potential for hiring new workers given its budget constraint. One cannot therefore hope to analyze the phenomenon of widening wage-gap in the LDCs without taking into account such market segmentation. In this chapter we examine the implications of such covered and uncovered labour markets. However, in doing so we deviate from the standard Harris-Todaro mechanism of migration and open urban unemployment. Following available empirical evidences that the low-skilled workers simply cannot afford to remain unemployed [Agenor (1996), Agenor and Montiel (1996), Mazumdar (1993)], we allow for unskilled labour to be fully employed even with two distinct wage rates. Those who do not get employment in the unionized formal segments, are absorbed in the informal sector through necessary decline of money wage.

Consider the same three-good framework as in Chapter 7 without the intermediate good. But suppose that the import-competing sector is dichotomized into formal and informal segments. These two segments produce different qualities of the import-competing good Y. In the formal segment, workers are recruited at the higher fixed wage, pre-determined by the trade union. In the informal segment, on the other hand, workers are hired at the market determined, flexible, low wage, W. To begin with, suppose capital can be borrowed in the market at the *same* rate by producers engaged in these segments. We shall return to the case of different borrowing cost later. With different wage-rental ratio, the input coefficients differ in the production processes in the formal and in the informal segments. We distinguish such coefficients for the informal-sector production activity by $\tilde{a}_{ij}$ from the input coefficients a_{ij} for the formal-sector production activity. In particular, production activity must be relatively capital intensive in the formal segment than that in the informal segment. Since high-quality varieties are typically more capital-intensive than the low-quality varieties, the formal segment would produce import-competing good of higher quality than the informal sector. As long as buyers are aware of the quality difference, world prices of these varieties will differ. We denote the world price of the low-quality good produced in the informal segment by $\tilde{P}_Y^*$.

The competitive product market conditions are assumed to prevail in both the formal and informal segments. Thus, given the world price of low-quality imports and an initial ad-valorem tariff, the zero-profit condition in the informal segment of the import-competing sector can be written as,

$$(1+t)\tilde{P}_Y^* = \tilde{P}_Y = \tilde{a}_{LY}W + \tilde{a}_{KY}r \tag{8.1}$$

This together with eqs. (7.1) - (7.3) in Chapter 7 constitute the price system of the model. Of course, in eq. (7.2) we must replace W by $\overline{W}$ because it is the zero-profit condition for the formal-segment of the import-competing sector. Note that, it has been assumed that agriculture is entirely an informal sector where unskilled workers are subject to low, market-determined wage just as their counterparts working in the informal segment of the manufacturing import-competing sector.

For the physical system, full employment conditions (7.5) and (7.6) need to be altered as well due to such coexistence of covered and uncovered labour markets. Denoting the informal sector production level by $\tilde{Y}$, we have,

$$\overline{K} = \tilde{a}_{KY}\tilde{Y} + a_{KY}Y + a_{KZ}Z \tag{8.2}$$

$$\overline{L} = \tilde{a}_{LY}\tilde{Y} + a_{LY}Y + a_{LX}X \tag{8.3}$$

Conditions (7.4) and (7.7) need not be changed, however.

With the coexistence of informal and formal labour markets, the policy-induced reallocation of labour across different sectors has quite different implications than otherwise. Contraction of the size of the informal sectors and *informalization* of the economy are generally viewed as indication of impoverishment of the unskilled working force. This is because such informalization implies displacement of labour from high-wage secured job to low-wage informal jobs with no or very little social security. However, that such inflow of labour from the formal sectors and consequent informalization of the economy lower unskilled-wage in the informal sector to make those initially employed there worse-off is not a foregone conclusion as is often believed. In fact, the Indian experience during its reform period indicates otherwise. According to both the National Sample Survey and the Ministry of Labour data reported in Shariff and Gumber (1999) and Acharyya and Marjit (2000b), real wage of the non-literate and unskilled workers has registered improvements between 1987-88 and 1993-94. Of late, Marjit (2000) has provided a simple theoretical explanation of a possible wage increase despite informalization. Essentially, this depends on the mobility of capital across informal and formal segments of the economy and on the nature of policy change that triggers the process of informalization.

To illustrate, consider the policy of import liberalization. Assume that only the import of high-quality product is liberalized. This is quite consistent with the policy changes introduced in India in its Export-Import policy 2000-2001. The quota restrictions are being replaced by less restricted tariffs but with quality regulations. In our set up, such an import policy affects the domestic price of the high-quality import-competing good produced in the formal segment, P_Y, but not that of the good produced in the informal segment, $\tilde{P}_Y$. The formal import-competing sector thus contracts and labour is displaced. With institutionally fixed money wage in the formal sector, the burden of adjustment is borne entirely by capital. As its return falls, labour is displaced further by the factor substitution effect. These workers flow into the informal segment. But with them flows capital as well. The informal sector thus expands. Since the rate of return to capital falls, the money wage must increase. It is interesting to observe that such a result is independent of the relative factor intensity ranking. In fact, Marjit and Beladi (2002) show that with wage-indexation in the formal sector, the Stolper-Samuelson result holds in this system without any assumption on factor intensity ranking. Note that as a consequence, unskilled labour will also be released from agriculture (which, in turn, contracts) thereby taking off some pressure on the money wage. But this cannot reverse the money wage increase in a *stable* equilibrium. Of course, this result depends on the possibility of capital mobility. We shall return to this shortly.

Do we have similar happy outcome when informalization takes place through liberalization of agricultural trade? Surprisingly, the real wage remains constant. Note that the segmentation of the import-competing sector into formal and informal sector alters the basic model of Chapter 7 in a very significant way. With the zero-profit condition for the informal segment constituting the fourth price equation of the system, the production structure becomes "as if" HOS. The factor prices are delinked from the full employment conditions and are uniquely determined by these price equations. Unlike in the basic model, the unskilled money wage together with the rate of return to capital are now tied down by the world prices of the two types of good Y that are produced in the formal and informal sectors at home. Thus as long as the informal manufacturing sector produces a traded good, a rise in price of agricultural good (following liberalization of agricultural trade) cannot affect the money wage of the unskilled workers because it is determined independent of its demand in agricultural production (as well as that in the informal manufacturing production).

The only effect of such price increase would be to raise the return to land more than proportionately and this makes room for expansion of agricultural production through substitution of relatively dearer land by unskilled labour. Overall, there would be a reallocation of unskilled labour from non-farm to agricultural employment. Interestingly such reverse flows of labour away from non-farm activities into agriculture have been observed in India in recent times after the reform programmes were initiated in 1991 [Bhalla (1997)].

Therefore, the following proposition is immediate from the above discussion :

Proposition 8.1: *Informalization of the economy raises the real wage of the unskilled workers when it takes place through contraction of the formal manufacturing sector. But the real wage falls when such a process of informalization is caused through agricultural trade liberalization.*

8.2 Informal Capital Market and Restricted Capital Mobility

It is well known in the literature on informal capital markets that returns to capital differ between formal and informal sectors. But, unlike the labour market, return to capital in the informal markets, dominated by few private moneylenders, is much higher than that in the formal markets where banks and financial intermediates operate. Of late, Aryytey et. al. (1997) discuss the issue in details and argue that oligopolistic nature of the capital market rather than greater risk of default explains such a premium. They also exhibit a clear positive relationship between formal and informal returns to capital. To incorporate this idea in the simplest possible way we assume that formal and informal sectors returns, r and $\tilde{r}$ respectively, are related in the following manner :

$$\tilde{r} = (1+\mu)r \tag{8.4}$$

where μ is the premium that is exogenously given. Thus, in (8.1) we replace r by $\tilde{r}$. Even if $\tilde{r} > r$, capital cannot freely flow towards the informal manufacturing sector. In effect this replicates the idea of an oligopolistic capital market where lenders are few and return is high. The premium μ varies with the degree market power of the agents in the informal credit market. Less imperfectly competitive the informal credit market is, lower is the premium on capital. Alternatively, we can think of such premium is due to imperfect capital mobility. Had there been perfect capital mobility across formal and informal sectors, either due to perfect competition in the respective credit markets or due to non-specificity of capital used in these sectors, the formal and informal rates of return to capital would have been the same. At the other extreme, if capital is sector-specific or immobile, the two rates are delinked from each other.

What implications do these have on the effect of informalization on unskilled wage? From (8.1) it is evident that informal unskilled money wage is affected only if the agricultural price affects the informal return to capital, $\tilde{r}$. But, if the premium on the return to capital is constant, r and $\tilde{r}$ must move together. Hence, the results stated in Proposition 8.1 above should not change. Therefore,

Proposition 8.2 : *For an exogenously given premium on return to capital, even with restricted mobility of capital across informal and formal segments of the manufacturing sector, effect of informalization of the economy on the unskilled money wage does not change qualitatively.*

But if capital is immobile across the formal and informal sectors, import-liberalization induced informalization lowers the unskilled-wage. The reason is simple. With such immobility of capital, the model becomes an extended specific-factor model with factor prices being no longer independent of the endowments. Now, for fixed capital stock in the informal sector, the movement of labour from the formal into the informal import-competing sector reduces the marginal product of labour there and hence lowers the informal unskilled-wage. Those who were locked in the informal sector suffer. Thus, the happy outcome for the insiders in the informal sector is not realized if capital cannot move out of the formal sector with labour and consequently the existing capital stock in the informal sector is overburdened with the workers displaced from the formal sector.

8.3 Role of the Non-Traded Good

It is well known by now that the existence of the non-traded goods, the market for which must clear *domestically*, significantly alter many standard results of the trade models. Since most of the non-traded production in the LDCs uses unskilled labour intensively, any discussion of changes in wage inequality in the LDCs through trade liberalization cannot be complete without such non-traded goods being taken into account. In Chapter 7, we incorporated a non-traded intermediate good. Here we examine the implications of a non-traded final good.

The more important issue, however, is the *nature* of such non-traded sectors. In particular, whether non-traded production is organized in the informal or in the formal sector may appear to be crucial. Essentially the way formal and informal sectors are modeled in the literature the issue at hand can be rephrased as examining the role of the non-traded production under alternative wage formation assumption: (higher) contractual unskilled-wage or fully flexible market-determined unskilled-wage. Since the traded sectors compete with the non-traded sectors for the scarce resources they commonly use and the non-traded production by definition must match its domestic demand, trade liberalization induced expansion of activities in the traded sectors will be possible only through a fall in the demand for non-tradable. This necessitates an increase in the price of non-traded goods and consequent changes in the domestic income distribution. Herein comes the role of the nature of the non-traded sector. If it is a formal sector with a contractual wage, the non-traded price may be determined solely by the cost of production independent of the demand for non-traded good. In such a case demand variation consequent upon trade liberalization induced real income changes alters only the non-traded production. Accordingly any change in the wage- gap is triggered by the consequent resource reallocation across the non-traded and traded sectors. But if the non-traded sector is an informal sector, variations in the demand for non-traded good are followed by the changes in both production and price of the non-traded good. Accordingly, trade liberalization will have quite different implications on the wage-gap between skilled and unskilled workers.

The purpose of this section is to focus on these issues. In particular, we examine the role of a non-traded sector in the context of the relationship between factor prices, wage inequality and trade liberalization. We consider the simple general equilibrium model developed above. The non-traded sector is modeled both as formal and informal sectors in turn. Unskilled workers who do not get jobs in the formal import-competing sector at the contractual wage are absorbed in the informal sector(s) at a lower (flexible) wage.

In this set up we observe that the production of goods that cannot be traded by itself alters the relationship between changes in wage inequality and trade liberalization significantly. On the other hand, when such non-traded good is produced in the *informal* segment of the economy, the *degree* of wage inequality changes compared to the case of formal-sector production of the non-traded good.

However, to highlight the role of non-traded good, we first spell out the link between trade liberalization and wage inequality with all "four" goods being internationally traded. Then it is indicated how the results are modified when one of these sectors is organized non-traded sector.

8.3.1 A Formal Non-Traded Sector

Consider a small open economy producing four goods. Production structures for the agricultural export good (X), manufacturing exports (Z) and manufacturing import-competing good (Y) are same as above. However, unlike in section 8.1 we assume that the import-competing good is produced only in the urban formal sector. In addition, the economy produces a non-traded good (N) using only unskilled labour in fixed proportion. This is, of course, only a simplifying assumption. In this section we assume that this non-traded good is produced in the formal sector where unskilled labour is hired at a contracted nominal wage. We will later consider implications of having the non-traded good produced in the informal sector. Thus, only the agricultural sector is modeled as the informal sector where the unskilled labour gets a lower market-determined nominal wage.

As usual all production is subject to constant returns to scale and except for the non-traded production there is diminishing returns to the variable factors in each sector. Given these assumptions, the zero-profit conditions for the sectors producing the three traded goods are reproduced below from Chapter 7 with relevant modifications :

$$P_X^* = a_{LX}W + a_{TX}R \tag{8.5}$$

$$P_Y = (1 + t) P_Y^* = a_{LY}\overline{W} + a_{KY}\, \mathbf{r} \tag{8.6}$$

$$P_Z^* = a_{SZ}W_S + a_{KZ}\, \mathbf{r} \tag{8.7}$$

The competitive condition for the non-traded good, on the other hand, is given by

$$P_N = a_{LN}\overline{W} \tag{8.8}$$

Flexibility of all factor prices (except the formal sector unskilled wage) guarantees full employment of the four factors of production and once again for convenience we reproduce them below :

$$\overline{T} = a_{TX}X \tag{8.9}$$

$$\overline{S} = a_{SZ}Z \tag{8.10}$$

$$\overline{K} = a_{KY}Y + a_{KZ}Z \tag{8.11}$$

$$\overline{L} = a_{LX}X + a_{LY}Y + a_{LN}N \tag{8.12}$$

The unskilled workers who do not find jobs in the formal sectors move to the informal agricultural sector and flexibility of nominal wage there ensures that all of them get absorbed there.

Finally, the market for non-traded good must clear domestically. With the simplifying assumption that α-proportion of the total urban income is spent on non-tradable and that the rural population does not have access to the urban non-traded output, this market-clearing condition can stated be as :

$$P_N N = \alpha[(a_{LY}Y + a_{LN}N)\, \overline{W} + W_S \overline{S} + r\overline{K}\,] \tag{8.13}$$

Note that once the non-traded market is cleared the overall trade is balanced.

The above set of nine equations solve for the nine variables --- four factor prices, (W_S, W, r, R), four output levels, (X, Z, Y, N), and the price of the non-traded good, P_N. Of course, there are the input choices, except the labour-nontradeables coefficient, which are determined once we know the factor prices.

The actual process of determination of equilibrium is as follows. Given the world price of the import good, and the ad-valorem tariff rate, t, the zero-profit condition there determines the rate of return to capital, r, which in turn determines the skilled-wage, W_S, from the zero-profit condition in the manufacturing export sector given its world price. On the other hand, the price of the non-traded good is given by the labour cost, which is the product of fixed input coefficient and the contracted unskilled-wage, independent of the demand for non-traded good. Once the skilled money wage and the rate of return to capital are known, total skilled labour force determines the manufacturing export production and this together with the total domestic capital stock gives us the production of the import-competing good. The non-traded output, on the other hand, is demand-determined given the equilibrium values of W_S, r and Y, as evident from the market-clearing condition (8.13)

Note that the formal sectors form an independent subsystem of the economy. The output and prices of the factors used in production of Z, Y and N are all determined independent of the informal agricultural sector[29]. But the wage rate, the return to land and the agricultural output level depend on the equilibrium values in the formal sectors of the economy. Since only those unskilled workers who are not employed in the formal import-competing and non-traded sectors at the higher contracted wage moves to the informal agriculture, it is obvious that its production activities will be constrained by the outputs and hence by the demand for unskilled labour in the formal sectors. Herein comes the role of the non-traded good. Had all goods been traded, production of agricultural exports would not necessarily be constrained by the demand for the non-traded good and the consequent demand for unskilled labour. Any excess demand would have been met through imports. Finally, given such an output level of the agricultural exports, informal sector wage and the return to the specific factor, land, must satisfy the zero-profit condition and full employment condition for land (8.9).

8.3.1.1 Trade Liberalization and Wage Inequality

Since the unskilled labour gets either the contracted wage, $\overline{W}$, in the formal sectors or a lower wage, W, in the informal agricultural sector, we define an average wage, ω, for our purpose :

---

[29] If we assume that a fraction of the rural income is spent on the non-traded good, the formal non-traded sector is no longer a part of the independent subsystem.

$$\omega \equiv \left(1 - \lambda_{LX}\right)\overline{W} + \lambda_{LX}W \tag{8.14}$$

where λ_{LX} is the share of agriculture in total employment of unskilled labour. Therefore, what we look at is the effect on e :

$$e \equiv \frac{\omega}{W_S} \tag{8.15}$$

An increase (decrease) in the value of e implies a declining (rising) wage-gap. However, as evident from (8.14), given this measure of wage inequality, not only changes in wage rates but also those in employment shares in the formal and informal sectors are important. In particular, if good-N is produced in the formal sector, the change in wage inequality can be decomposed as :

$$\hat{e} = \left[\frac{1}{\omega}(\overline{W} - \omega)(d\lambda_{LY} + d\lambda_{LN}) + \delta\hat{W}\right] - \hat{W}_S \tag{8.16}$$

where $\delta \equiv \dfrac{\lambda_{LX}W}{(1 - \lambda_{LX})\overline{W} + \lambda_{LX}W}$.

But when good-N is produced in the informal sector, the decomposition changes to,

$$\hat{e} = \left[\frac{1}{\omega'}(\overline{W} - W)d\lambda_{LY} + \delta'\hat{W}\right] - \hat{W}_S \tag{8.17}$$

where $\delta'' \equiv \dfrac{(1 - \lambda_{LY})W}{\lambda_{LY}\overline{W} + (1 - \lambda_{LY})W}$ and $\omega' \equiv \lambda_{LY}\overline{W} + (1 - \lambda_{LY})W$.

Given such measures of wage inequality, we now proceed to examine the implications of trade liberalization. Though (multilateral) trade liberalization should imply simultaneous price changes, to fix ideas we consider the effects of each of these changes one at a time.

To highlight the role of the non-traded good, let us begin with the trade and factor-price relationship when all goods are traded. Thus, with good-N being traded as well in this exercise, the model specified above boils down to standard 4x4 HO model. Note that eq. (8.13) is now redundant because once the four factor prices are determined from competitive price equations, full employment conditions determine the output levels independent of domestic demand for the goods. However, with only unskilled labour being used to produce good-N, we must assume this sector as informal sector so that producers can hire unskilled labour at market determined flexible money wage. With such modification, effect of trade liberalization on factor prices and wage inequality is summarized in Table 8.1. The proofs are simple and are avoided here.

The interesting point to observe is that despite an increase in world price of agricultural good, the unskilled-wage being tied down by the world price of good-N, unskilled workers do not gain. Skilled workers gain neither, leaving the wage inequality (as well as the standard measure of wage-gap indicated in column 6) unchanged. On the other hand, if good-N is imported, fall in its price reduces the wage inequality.

Table 8.1

Effect on Factor Prices: All Goods are Traded

Initial	Change in					
Shock	W_S	W	r	R	W/W_S	e
Fall in P_Y	+	0	-	0	-	-
Rise in P_X	0	0	0	+	0	0
Rise in P_Z	+	0	0	0	-	-

With these effects at hand, we now refer back to our model specified earlier with good-N being not traded, and reexamine the relationship between trade liberalization and wage inequality. To begin with we assume non-traded good is produced in the formal sector of the economy. Later we shall explore the other case.

I. *Import Liberalization* :

The immediate impact of a tariff cut is to reduce the rate of return to capital and consequently to raise the skilled-wage as evident from the zero-profit conditions (8.6) and (8.7). How does the informal unskilled-wage change? It depends on whether the formal sectors that use unskilled workers, contracts or not. Formally,

$$\frac{\sigma_X \lambda_{LX}}{\theta_{TX}} \hat{W} = \lambda_{LY}(\sigma_Y \hat{P}_Y + \hat{Y}) + \lambda_{LN}\hat{N} \tag{8.18}$$

The left hand side in (8.18) measures the change in labour demand in the informal sector due to the input substitution effect. But this is an induced effect of the change in unskilled-wage. If the demand for the unskilled labour in the rest of the economy, as measured by the right hand side of (8.18), does not change there is no reason why the unskilled-wage should change. Accordingly, with the world price of the agricultural good not changing in this instance, the factor price ratio in agriculture, W/R, and hence the unskilled labour-land ratio will remain unchanged. Therefore, there would be no change in total demand for unskilled labour and consequently no change in the informal unskilled-wage implying a widening wage-gap. Whether this is the case depends on how the productions of import-competing and non-traded goods are changing and on the input substitution effect in the import-competing sector. The first term on the right hand side captures the fall in labour demand due to substitution of relatively cheaper capital for labour following import liberalization. There is also a fall in demand for unskilled labour on account of the contraction of the import-competing sector measured by the second term. The import-competing sector contracts on two accounts. First, an expansion of the manufacturing export production through substitution of skilled labour by cheaper capital necessitates release of scarce domestic capital from the import-competing sector.

Second, with the wage-rental ratio, $\overline{W}/r$, going down, more capital-intensive technique is employed to produce the import-competing good which lowers output for any given allocation of the capital stock. Therefore, informal sector wage unambiguously falls if the non-traded sector contracts as well thereby adding to the pool of released unskilled labour. And this is exactly what happens to be the case.

With such a fall in the unskilled money wage, and contraction of the formal import-competing and non-traded sectors, the wage-gap unambiguously widens. Hence,

Proposition 8.3: *In the above set up with a formal non-traded sector, import liberalization unambiguously raises wage inequality.*

A formal proof is provided in the appendix.

At this point it is instructive to look at how the informal-sector employment changes and unskilled workers are reallocated across the formal and informal sectors of the economy. Since in the above set up only agriculture constitutes the informal sector employment, so all we have to examine is how the agricultural employment, denoted by L_X, changes. Since $L_X = a_{LX}X$ so,

$$\hat{L}_X = \hat{a}_{LX} + \hat{X}$$

Hence, solving for the output change from the percentage change form of (8.9) and using $\hat{R} = -\dfrac{\theta_{LX}}{\theta_{TX}}\hat{W}$, this boils down to:

$$\hat{L}_e = -\frac{\sigma_X}{\theta_{TX}}\hat{W} > 0 \tag{8.19}$$

since by (8.18), unskilled money wage falls.

Thus, more people now work in the informal sector at a lower wage. This indicates greater impoverishment of the unskilled workforce than just a fall in their money wage. In fact this is captured in the above index of average wage for the unskilled workers defined in (8.15).

II. *Increase in the World Price of Agricultural Exports*

How does multilateral trade liberalization, leading to an increase in the world price of the agricultural export for this small open economy, affect the degree of wage inequality? First of all, note that with the unchanged world price of imports and the tariff rate, the rate of return to capital and consequently skill wage do not change. Accordingly there will be no input substitution effect through which the manufacturing export production (Z) and import-competing production (Y) can change. On the other hand, with the price of the non-traded good dragged down by the contractual wage payments, non-traded output also cannot change since the urban income and hence the demand for non-traded good are unchanged. This is obvious because the formal sectors in this set up constitute the independent subsystem and accordingly any parametric changes in the informal agricultural sector will leave these sectors undisturbed. Consequently the agricultural export sector can expand following the increase in the world price only by using labour less intensively and land more intensively. But given fixed endowment of land specific to this sector this is not possible. Therefore, the only effect will be proportional increases in the unskilled wage and the return to land with *no real effect*. Hence,

Proposition 8.4: *In the above set up with a formal non-traded sector, an increase in the world price of agricultural good unambiguously reduces wage inequality.*

However, as we will show later, if the non-traded good is produced in the informal sector, changes in the unskilled-wage will affect the price of the non-traded good as well which in turn affects the non-traded production even if the urban income remains constant. Accordingly, the unskilled-wage will be affected further.

III. *An Increase in the World Price of Manufacturing Exports*

An increase in the price of the manufacturing exports, unlike the previous case, will have some real effects. The immediate impact will be an increase in the skilled-wage and with the rate of return to capital held fixed by the given world price of importable and the ad-valorem tariff rate, such increase will be more than proportionate. Consequently input substitution effect will raise production of manufacturing exports. This causes output of the import-competing good to fall since some capital is withdrawn to support the additional production of the Z-good. But the change in urban income and consequently the demand for non-traded good are ambiguous. In particular, it is straightforward to check that the change in output of the non-traded good equals,

$$\hat{N} = \frac{\sigma_Z}{\theta_{SZ}}\left[-\gamma\frac{\lambda_{KZ}}{\lambda_{KY}} + (1-\gamma)\theta_{KZ}\right]\hat{P}_Z^* + (1-\gamma)\hat{P}_Z^* \tag{8.20}$$

The first term in the parenthesis is negative for similar reason which ensured an increase in production of the non-traded good earlier in case of import liberalization (see appendix). Therefore, in this case $\hat{N}$ can be of either sign. If non-traded production falls, some unskilled labour will be released from this sector as well along with that from the import-competing sector and accordingly the unskilled wage must fall to absorb them in the informal agriculture. But if non-traded production increases, not significantly though, some of the released unskilled labour will be absorbed in the non-traded sector thereby necessitating much smaller wage fall in the informal agricultural sector. In either case, the wage-gap widens. It is only when non-traded production increases significantly, requiring more unskilled labour than are released by the contracting import-competing sector, the unskilled wage will go up and wage-gap *may* decline consequent upon such (net) excess demand for unskilled labour in the formal sector as a whole. Therefore,

Proposition 8.5: *For a small open economy with a formal non-traded sector, an increase in the world price of its manufacturing exports may lower the degree of wage inequality. A necessary condition for this is that the non-traded sector must expand along with the manufacturing export sector.*

8.3.2 Informalization of the Non-Traded Sector

So far we have considered a formal non-traded sector. One implication of this assumption is that the non-traded price is held fixed by the contracted unskilled-wage. But in case of non-traded good being produced in the informal sector where unskilled labour is paid the market-determined (flexible) money wage, non-traded output is no longer demand-determined. Similarly, the non-traded price is not just cost-determined.

With the informal sector production of the non-traded good, the zero-profit condition (8.8) now must be rewritten as :

$$P_N = a_{LN}W \tag{8.8a}$$

The prices and outputs in the formal sectors, Y and Z, can still be determined independent of the informal sectors, N and X. The rest of the variables are determined in the following way. For any given P_N, (8.8a) determines the unskilled wage, W, which in turn determines the return to land, R, from the zero-profit condition (8.5). Given these. factor prices along with the consequent input choices, the output levels of the agricultural exports and non-traded good, X and N, are determined from (8.9) and (8.12) respectively. This describes a supply relationship for the non-traded good : $N^s = \varphi^s(P_N)$. An increase in P_N raises W and lowers R; the consequent increase in intensity of land use lowers the agricultural output which along with the less intensive use of unskilled labour due to the higher unskilled-wage releases some unskilled labour; accordingly the non-traded output increases. We, therefore, have a positive association between P_N and N^s. On the other hand, rewriting (8.13) as

$$\alpha\left[(1+t)P_Y^*Y + P_Z^*\right] = (1-\alpha)P_N N \qquad (8.13a)$$

it appears that the demand curve for the non-traded good is a rectangular hyperbola. Therefore, the equilibrium price and output of non-traded good are determined by the equality of supply and demand relationships as illustrated in Figure 8.1.

This interplay of demand for and supply of non-traded good in determining its price and output levels has far reaching implications on the wage-gap between skilled and unskilled labour. Given (8.8a), i.e., proportionality between the non-traded price and the unskilled money wage, it is immediate that whether the wage-gap widens or declines following trade liberalization depends crucially on the movement of the non-traded price. In the previous case of the formal non-traded sector it was only the demand-determined non-traded output which was crucial. But now with the price of non-traded good no longer determined by the contracted unskilled money wage, supply of non-traded good is no less important in determining the movement in unskilled-wage.

Consider first the case of import liberalization. At the initial P_N, this unambiguously lowers the urban income and consequently the demand for non-traded good. That is, the demand curve in Figure 8.1 shifts to the left. The consequent excess supply puts a downward pressure on P_N. How is the supply of non-traded good affected? At the initial P_N and hence W and X, a fall in the production of the import-competing good as well as less intensive use of unskilled labour in such production due to fall in rate of return to capital, relaxes the (net) labour constraint for the non-traded sector thereby raising its production. Thus, the supply curve in Figure 8.1 shifts to the right reinforcing the excess supply consequent upon the demand fall and the price of the non-traded good falls unambiguously. Therefore,

Proposition 8.6: *With an informal non-traded sector, import liberalization by a small open economy increases the degree of wage inequality relative to that with a formal non-traded sector.*

When the non-traded good is produced in the formal sector there would be no supply effect since the non-traded price is tied to the contracted unskilled-wage. That is, the fall in unskilled-wage and the consequent widening of the wage-gap are caused only by the fall in non-traded demand through fall in urban income. But in case of the informally produced non-traded good, we have a supply effect too which reinforces fall in unskilled-wage and hence magnifies the widening wage-gap.

The case of an increase in the world price of agricultural exports may similarly be worked out. As explained earlier, at the initial P_N , there will be no change in the demand for non-traded since the urban income is determined independent of the informal agricultural sector. The proportional increase in the unskilled-wage consequent upon the increase in the world price, as explained earlier, will however trigger a supply effect: Given (8.8a), the non-traded price will increase proportionately, i.e., the supply curve in Figure 8.1 will shift up. The consequent contraction of the non-traded sector will release some unskilled labour which in turn will dampen the initial (proportional) increase in unskilled-wage. In other words, due to the supply-effect the decline in the wage-gap will not be as large as it is in case of non-traded good produced in the formal sector. Note that, the increase in the price of agricultural export good will now have a real effect which in fact makes the increase in the unskilled-wage less than proportional.

On the other hand, when the world price of the manufacturing exports increases, the demand effect on the non-traded price is given by (8.20). But the price of the non-traded good now may move in either direction. On the other hand, the supply-effect depresses the non-traded price : At the initial P_N and hence at the initial W and X, unskilled labour released from the contracting import-competing sector relaxes the (net) labour constraint for the non-traded sector and thereby raises its supply. The net change in non-traded price is, therefore, ambiguous. But what is to be noted that the additional supply effect lowers the unskilled-wage. Thus, if in case of formal sector production the wage inequality increased (declined), it will now be magnified (dampened).

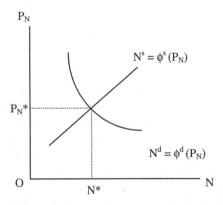

Figure 8.1: Informal Non-Traded Market

To summarize, an informal sector does have a perceptible influence on the effect of trade liberalization on wage inequality. Though the direction of changes in wage inequality is not affected much, the degree such inequality is quite different depending upon whether the non-traded good is produced in the formal or informal sector. Informally produced non-traded goods makes the unskilled workers more vulnerable to liberal trade policies.

The role of existence non-traded good is evident from Table 8.2. Whereas, import liberalization by the South has the same adverse effect on the wage inequality as that when good-N is traded, in other cases, the relationship between trade and wage inequality gets altered significantly.

Table 8.2

Trade and Wage Inequality: Role of the Non-Traded Good

Initial Shock	Good-N is Traded	Good N is Non-Traded	
		Formal Sector	Informal Sector
$\hat{P}_Y < 0$	$\hat{e} < 0$	$\hat{e} < 0$ and magnified	$\hat{e} < 0$ and magnified further
$\hat{P}_X^* > 0$	$\hat{e} = 0$	$\hat{e} > 0$	$\hat{e} > 0$ but smaller
$\hat{P}_Z^* > 0$	$\hat{e} < 0$	a. $\hat{e} < 0$ & magnified if $\hat{N} < 0$ b. $\hat{e} >$ or < 0 if $\hat{N} < 0$	$\hat{e} >$ or < 0 smaller if $\hat{e} > 0$ larger if $\hat{e} < 0$

8.4 Conclusion

Covered and uncovered input markets may have far reaching implications for the trade and wage-gap nexus. Coexistence of such markets, particularly in the manufacturing sectors, is a typical feature of the developing countries. It is important to note that in such a context a boost in agricultural exports through world market boom may in fact worsen the position of unskilled workers in real terms. Capital mobility between the formal and informal segments of the manufacturing sector also plays a crucial role. It is important to understand these relationships in order to formulate policies aimed at improving the position of the unskilled workers.

We have also examined the role of a non-traded sector in terms of a simple four sector general equilibrium model consistent with diversified trade patterns and production structures of many developing countries. We find that whereas the import liberalization indeed causes the wage-gap between skilled and unskilled labour and hence wage inequality to increase, improvement in the terms of trade through the increase in the world price of exports depend upon the nature of the export good. For an increase in the price of the manufacturing exports, that does not use unskilled labour, the wage-gap may in fact decline through a sufficiently large increase in the demand for and output of the non-traded good. Herein lies the role of the non-traded good. On the other hand, if the price increase is for the agricultural export good using unskilled labour, the wage-gap unambiguously falls. Moreover, the extent of trade induced wage-gap depends on whether the non-traded good is produced in the formal or informal sector.

The informality of the non-traded sector by itself makes quite significant differences. It either magnifies wage inequality (as in case of import liberalization) or dampens the improvement in the relative position of the unskilled labour (as in case of increase in world price of agricultural exports). In either case, it works against the interest of the unskilled labour. Since the informal sectors are a major source of employment for unskilled workers in the developing economies, these results have far reaching implications for policy-making in these countries. Furthermore, it can be easily verified that these results do not change qualitatively if we allow capital mobility across the non-traded and formal traded sectors.

APPENDIX

Proof of Proposition 8.3

From (8.17) in the text it is evident that since $d\lambda_{LY} < 0$ in this case and $\overline{W} > \omega$, given (8.19), a sufficient condition for wage inequality to rise ($\hat{e}$) is $d\lambda_{LN} < 0$. But $\lambda_{LN} = a_{LN}N/L$. Since a_{LN} is fixed by assumption, this requires a contraction of the non-traded sector.

Consider the percentage change form of (8.13a) in the text :

$$\gamma(\hat{Y} + \hat{P}_Y) + (1-\gamma)\hat{Z} = \hat{N} \qquad (A.8.1)$$

where,

$$\gamma \equiv \frac{\alpha(1+t)P_Y^*Y}{(1-\alpha)P_N N} \quad \text{and} \quad (1-\gamma) \equiv \frac{\alpha P_Z^* Z}{(1-\alpha)P_N N}$$

Thus the change in non-traded production depends on the change in the output of manufacturing export and import-competing goods. From (8.10),

$$\hat{Z} = -\hat{a}_{KZ} \tag{A.8.2}$$

Now by the least-cost input combination rule, $\theta_{SZ}\hat{a}_{SZ} + \theta_{KZ}\hat{a}_{KZ} = 0$, and by definition of the factor-substitution elasticity in the Z-sector, $\sigma_Z(\hat{W}_S - \hat{r}) = \hat{a}_{KZ} - \hat{a}_{SZ}$. But,

$$\hat{W}_S = -\frac{\theta_{KZ}}{\theta_{SZ}\theta_{KY}}\hat{P}_Y \quad \text{and} \quad \hat{r} = \frac{1}{\theta_{KY}}\hat{P}_Y$$

Hence, (A.8.2) boils down to,

$$\hat{Z} = -\frac{\sigma_Z\theta_{KZ}}{\theta_{SZ}\theta_{KY}}\hat{P}_Y > 0 \tag{A.8.3}$$

Thus, tariff reduction raises the output of skill-intensive manufacture. On the other hand, by (8.11),

$$\lambda_{KY}(\hat{a}_{KY} + \hat{Y}) + \lambda_{KZ}(\hat{a}_{KZ} - \hat{a}_{SZ}) = 0 \tag{A.8.4}$$

Once again by the least-cost rule in this sector and the definition of factor-substitution elasticity,

$$\hat{a}_{KY} = -\frac{\sigma_Y\theta_{LY}}{\theta_{KY}}\hat{P}_Y$$

Therefore, substitution of this and the definition of σ_Z in (A.8.4), yields the change in production of the import-competing good as,

$$\hat{Y} = -\left[\frac{\sigma_Y\theta_{LY}}{\theta_{KY}} + \frac{\sigma_Z\lambda_{KZ}}{\lambda_{KY}\theta_{SZ}\theta_{KY}}\right]\hat{P}_Y < 0 \tag{A.8.5}$$

Combining (A.8.1), (A.8.4) and (A.8.6) we get,

$$\tilde{N} = -\left[\frac{\gamma(\sigma_Y\theta_{LY} + \theta_{KY})}{\theta_{KY}} + \frac{\sigma_Z\{\gamma\lambda_{KZ} - (1-\gamma)\lambda_{KY}\theta_{KZ}\}}{\lambda_{KY}\theta_{KY}\theta_{SZ}}\right]\hat{P}_Y \tag{A.8.6}$$

Consider the numerator of the second term on the right hand side of (A.8.6),

$$\sigma_Z\{\gamma\lambda_{KZ} - (1-\gamma)\lambda_{KY}\theta_{KZ}\} = \frac{\alpha\sigma_Z a_{KZ}YZ}{\overline{K}(1-\alpha)P_N N}(P_Y - a_{KY}r)$$

But this is positive by (8.6) in the text. Therefore, the term in the parenthesis is positive and accordingly production of the non-traded good falls. Hence the claim.

9 TRADE, SKILL FORMATION AND THE WAGE-GAP

9.1 Introduction

In the theoretical analyses of the earlier chapters the focus has been on the wage inequality between skilled and unskilled at a very aggregate level instead of on the changes in wage inequality among workers of different skills or abilities. But intra-skill wage distribution can easily be a separate focal point for research in the current context. In Chile, for example, the wage-gap between workers with university degree and with secondary education (measured by their wage ratio) has been more pronounced than that between workers with university degree and with primary education for all age groups (see Table 2.4). In India, on the other hand, the wage-gap between graduates and non-literates has in fact declined in the manufacturing sector during 1987-94 (see Table 2.6). The middle-aged Chilean workers with university degree had similar experience of declining wage-gap vis-à-vis those with secondary education. These small but curious pieces of evidence seem to deserve some theoretical attention. At the same time, almost all-round growing wage inequality in Chile across skills, however asymmetric that may be, and somewhat mixed experience in India, warrant different explanations for the possible underlying causes.

Section 9.2 of this chapter provides a simple theoretical explanation of these phenomena in terms of a general equilibrium model with unionized activity and continuum of skill-differentiated workers. We show that the trade story seems to be quite appropriate for the Indian experience. On the other hand, the argument put forward by Edwards and Edwards (1995) and Wood (1997) that curtailment of union power and lowering of minimum wage in Chile in the late 1970s caused the wage-gap to widen there in the 1980s, fits well with our theoretical explanation for Chile.

The general equilibrium structure, elaborated upon Marjit and Beladi (2000) and Acharyya and Marjit (2001), also creates a scope for analyzing effects on underemployment. Substantial underemployment instead of open unemployment in many developing countries has been documented in Agenor (1996). We identify underemployed as essentially those who do not get employment in the unionized industrial sectors and are forced to migrate to the informal sectors and *involuntarily self-employed* in agriculture.

An overpowering consequence of globalization for the developing countries is its impact on the internal demand for and supply of skill. Increasing trade and investment requires specialized skills which may be in short supply in a developing country. Hence, one would expect that with the expansion of trade, the process of skill formation would also get a natural boost increasing the knowledge base of the economy which in turn will have growth enhancing effects. In section 9.3 we focus on this process of skill formation and its implications on the wage inequality.

However, the simple story of positive correlation between trade and increased skill formation tends to overlook a number of possibilities. The supply of skill may take a long time to respond to growing demand particularly in countries where basic education is yet to flourish in a significant scale. The effect of a greater demand for skill may enlarge the skilled and unskilled wage-gap to a much greater extent in a developing country than in a more affluent nation where skill is easier to acquire. We shall demonstrate such a possibility in section 9.3.1 by constituting a suitable general equilibrium model in which skill is interpreted as an intermediate input made of unskilled labour and capital. Theoretical correlation between skilled-unskilled wage and price of the traded goods is studied by explicitly taking into account endogenous formation of skill. In a way it supplements our analyses in Chapter 7 by re-exploring the commodity price-factor price relationship when skill can be explicitly acquired and capital is utilized both for production and skill formation.

Paradoxical it may seem, but the fact is that it may be of national interest of a welfare state to limit skill formation and inflow of skilled labour in its export sector. China is a vivid example in this regard that restricted labour mobility into its export processing zone. Thus, maintaining a wage-gap may be socially optimum. Following Marjit and Beladi (1997a), we elaborate upon this issue in section 9.3.2.

The simpler framework then gives way to a more complex description of skill formation in section 9.3.3 where acquiring human capital requires a threshold level of physical capital which in turn is unevenly distributed. Given other use of capital, people may not like to invest in education. Liberal trade policies may alter the process of skill formation and wage distribution in an interesting way. It is possible that only some affluent ones get increasing opportunity of upgrading skills. Deregulation, liberalization or increasing degree of integration with the rest of the world do create expanding opportunities for the talented and skilled people. The contribution of such a process should not be undermined. But the major problem can still be the one which does not allow a significant chunk of the population to avail of these global opportunities. Basic education and financial capabilities to tap on the benefits of the process and expand along with the growth may still not be available to a large number of people and therefore the process may entail a fairly long phase of sustained and possibly growing inequality. A glimpse of such an outcome is sought to be captured through a theoretical framework which tries to extend the simpler model with no assumption on the initial distribution of investible capital on skill formation. We rule out borrowing or lending in our model because to us it is a pertinent assumption that collateralization of human capital is not a common phenomenon in the developing countries. Also the financial statements of banks and other financial institutions will have less than minuscule proportion of the funding going for investment in human capital. What we suggest in terms of a simple expository general equilibrium model is that financial or wealth constraint operating on the ability to form human capital, may worsen the wage distribution. In fact, more unequal wage distribution reduces the possibility of a *poverty trap* in the standard model of distribution and development such as in Gal-or and Zeira (1992). Greater initial inequality increases the incentives to acquire skill and therefore can rule out low-level equilibrium in an otherwise multiple equilibrium framework. This is something that may bother a few who think that a large number of people in poor countries may not have the power, however defined, to respond to such increasing incentives. Although in models of Gal-or and Zeira (1992) and Banerjee and Newman (1993) the initial distribution dictate the pattern of long run achievements, initial wage-gap has a positive impact on the eventual equilibrium configuration. This is due to the fact that a greater wage-gap increases the return from acquiring skills and therefore expands the size of the skilled population. But the focus of our analysis is on the wage-gap itself. The problem of income distribution is magnified through the existence of an imperfect credit market and indivisibility of investment in human capital. A critical minimum level of investment may be required for acquiring skill that has the potential of fetching a considerably high rate of return. Interestingly, even without explicit alleviation of imperfection in the credit market one can conceive of a drastic decline in such a critical minimum level of investment. This has to do with the process of fragmentation in international trade. As discussed earlier in Chapter 7, Jones and Kierzkowski (2001) argue that specialization in fragments of a given production process must reduce the requirement of capital for production. In fact, higher return to specialized skills can be derived because fragments of product may require much less start up cost than in a situation where some vertically integrated processes are produced locally and traded internationally. We try to incorporate this idea in our analysis of skill formation and wage-gap in section 9.3.3.

9.2 Skill Differentiation, Underemployment and Wage Inequality

9.2.1 The Scenario

Consider workers in a small open economy with three broad levels of education received : Graduates and above (G); secondary degree holders (S); and those having at most primary education (P). The level of skill of a worker varies with his level of education. But there might be variations of skills or productivity even among a particular education group. All MBA graduates may not have same level of skill or productivity. Similarly it is not unusual to find production workers or artisans having same level of education but different levels of skills. To incorporate such variability of skill across education levels as well as among workers with same level of education, we differentiate workers by their level of skill indexed by $q \in [0, \bar{q}]$. Let, intervals $[0, q^P]$, $[q^P, q^S]$, and $[q^S, \bar{q}]$ denote range of skills of workers having primary education, secondary education and college education and above, respectively.

There are two sectors in the economy: a unionized sector where an import-competing good Y is produced using labour at a fixed money wage $\bar{W}$ and capital, and an export sector where workers are self employed. In the import-competing sector though production technology requires a minimum skill or education level, variability in productivity of labour above that level has no impact on output in this sector. Capital is the all important factor of production. To be more precise, let labour with at least secondary education, having skill $q \in [q^P, \bar{q}]$, can be combined with capital to produce the good. Highly capital-intensive manufacturing good with a standardized production technology is a typical example[30].

In the export sector there are two types of production activities. One is the relatively highly-skilled and educated labour intensive activities (Z) like software development or consultancy services. The other is the category of low-skill intensive activities (X) like leather and textile manufacturing, that require labour having just primary education. Thus whereas workers having at least graduate level of education and consequently having $q \in [q^S, \bar{q}]$ are engaged in high-skill export activity, others having skill $q \in [0, q^S]$ may be engaged in production of the low-skill export good. As pointed out earlier, this diverse export basket of both low-skill and high-skill products, fits well for India and more or less for many other developing countries. People engaged in both sectors are self-employed small entrepreneurs with their productivity and skill influencing their return.

Both the activities in the export sector have fixed coefficient technology. Each self-employed worker hires one unit of capital and produces $1/a(q)$ units of the export good. The level of output these workers produce, therefore, depends upon their productivity or skill.

The assumption regarding the input-output ratio that we make is the following :

$$a(0) = \infty, a'(q) < 0, a''(q) < 0, a'(q) \to 0 \text{ as } q \to \bar{q} \tag{9.1}$$

These are fairly standard assumptions indicating that the marginal product of labour increases but at a decreasing rate with the level of skill. The restriction on

---

[30] For India, in particular, highly capital-intensive manufacturing goods (for example, white goods or their components) still constitute major import items.

the marginal product at the limit, on the other hand, guarantees that equilibrium exists in a sense spelled out later.

Note that here labour is partially mobile in the sense that while graduates can perform all the jobs and thus can move around wherever they get higher returns, the workers with secondary education and corresponding skill levels defined above, can move only between the import-competing sector (Y) and the low-skilled export activity (X). The workers with primary education are, on the other hand, specific to the low-skilled export activity. The money wage in the export sector is fully flexible and, as we will see later, varies for each self-employed worker with his level of skill. In the import competing sector, on the other hand, the money wage is set by the union regardless of the productivity differences of the workforce employed there.

Since the country is assumed to be small, we set the given set of world prices of the two export goods and the import good to unity. With an initial ad-valorem tariff at the rate t, the competitive price conditions can be written as,

$$(1 + t) = a_{LY}\overline{W} + a_{KY}r \tag{9.2}$$

$$1 = a(q)[W + r] \tag{9.3}$$

Since each labour produces $1/a(q)$ units of the export good using one unit of capital, capital used per unit of the good is also $a(q)$ and hence the average capital cost is $a(q)r$. Moreover, since production technologies for both the high-skilled and the low-skilled activities are assumed to be same, eq. (9.3) describes the zero-profit condition for both these activities. The essential difference between these activities is the specific skill(s) required to perform the activities. This has been incorporated in the input coefficient, $a(q)$, which, for any given rate of return to capital, leads to differential money return both across these activities as well as within each activity.

Formally, from (9.3) a little manipulation yields :

$$W = \frac{1 - a(q)r}{a(q)} = W(q), \; W_q > 0 \tag{9.4}$$

Such a wage curve is shown in Figure 9.1. Thus given our assumed skill (or education) specificity in the two types of export activities, and the monotonicity of the $W(q)$ function, graduates with skill levels $q \in [q^S, \overline{q}]$, engaged in production of the high-skilled export good (Z), earn higher money wage than primary degree holders with skill levels $q \in [q^P, \overline{q}]$, engaged in production of the low-skilled export good (Y). At the same time, each worker gets differential money return (or rent) from their self-employment in the same activity due to their skill differences.

The model displays the Heckscher-Ohlin property: Factor prices are determined regardless of factor endowments. For a given ad-valorem tariff rate (t) and the rigid money wage in the import-competing sector, the above set of price equations, along with the input choices for production of the import-competing good, $a_{iX} = a_{iX}(\overline{W}, r)$, determine the two factor prices, W and r, and the input coefficients, a_{iX}.

Productions of the high-skilled export good (Z), low-skilled export good (X) and the import-competing good (Y) are constrained by the availability of the total stock of capital. Since by the assumed technology, each self-employed labour in the export sector hires one unit of capital, capital stock used up in this sector is just the number of workers self-employed there (i.e., $L_Z + L_X$). Thus,

$$\overline{K} = L_Z + L_X + a_{KY}Y \tag{9.5}$$

On the other hand, the workforce engaged in production of the high-skilled export good cannot exceed the total number of graduates, $\left(\overline{q} - q^S\right)$:

$$L_Z \leq \int_{q^S}^{\overline{q}} dq = \left(\overline{q} - q^S\right) \tag{9.6}$$

Of course, all graduates may not be self-employed in the Z-sector, and might seek job in the unionized import-competing sector. We shall return to such a decision shortly. Total availability of labour for the production of the import competing good (Y) and the low-skilled export good (X) is, therefore, $\overline{L} - L_Z$:

$$\overline{L} - L_Z = a_{LY}Y + L_X \tag{9.7}$$

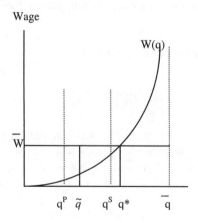

Figure 9.1: Allocation of Skill

What is the level of production of the low-skilled export good, X, and the number of self-employed workers, L_X, there? All workers having at most primary level of education must be self-employed there. These are the $\int_0^{q^P} dq \equiv q^P$ number of people, (i.e., $L_X = q^P$), and given the technology, the total production would be X_P,

$$X = X_P = \int_0^{q^P} \frac{1}{a(q)} dq \qquad \text{if} \quad \overline{L} - L_Z - q^P = a_{LY} Y \qquad (9.8a)$$

But actual production of the good may be even larger if the net capital stock available for production of the import-competing good, $\overline{K} - L_Z - q^P$, does not permit all secondary degree holders (and possibly some of the graduates who choose to work in this sector) to be absorbed there. This is the other possibility as defined in (9.8b) below :

$$X = \tilde{X} = \int_0^{q^P} \frac{1}{a(q)} dq + \delta \qquad \text{if} \quad \overline{L} - L_Z - q^P > a_{LY} Y \qquad (9.8b)$$

However, how many of those workers will fall back upon the low-skilled export sector and consequently how much additional production of X will take place (i.e., what will be the value of δ), depend on the number of graduates choose to be self-employed in the high-skilled export sector (Z) and the hiring scheme in the unionized import-competing sector. To this we now turn.

Graduates, with skill levels $q \in [q^S, \overline{q}]$, can earn $W(q)$ according to (9.4) if they are self-employed in the export sector. Alternatively, they can earn the fixed money wage, by working in the import-competing sector. Obviously, they will be self-employed if $W(q) > \overline{W}$. Now define a worker with ability q^* is such that,

$$\overline{W} = W(q^*) \qquad (9.9)$$

Since, by (9.4), $W_q > 0$, workers with skill levels $q > q^*$ would be willing to work in the unionized import-competing sector. Note that the restriction on $a'(q)$ defined in (9.1), ensures that such a $q^* < \overline{q}$ exists[31]. This means, for any fixed money wage in the unionized sector, there is always some workers who would be voluntarily self-employed in the high-skilled export sector. Moreover, suppose $\overline{W}$ is such that $q^* > q^S$. That is, we assume that not all graduates will be willing to be self-employed. In particular, by our assumption, $L_Z = \overline{q} - q^* < \overline{q} - q^S$. Graduates with skill levels $q \in [q^S, \overline{q}]$, will, therefore, seek jobs in the unionized

---

[31] Of course, we must assume that $W(q)$ is continuous. The monotonicity and single-valuedness of $W(q)$, on the other hand, guarantee that q^* is unique.

import-competing sector since it offers a higher money wage. Of course, all secondary degree holders will also be willing to work there.

Do all the $(q* - q^P)$ number of people willing to work in the unionized sector get absorbed there? This depends on the net capital available for production of the import-competing good as spelled out above. In particular, the level of unionized wage in the import-competing manufacturing sector and the productivity of workers in the agricultural sector are the important factors determining this. Abstracting from the algebraic details, in general, we can expect that for a very high unionized wage, $a_{LY}Y < (q* - q^P)$. We confine ourselves with this case in rest of the analysis. Thus a few workers are forced to fall back upon the export sector.

Given such a state of excess supply of labour, how the workers in the unionized sector are hired from amongst those willing to work? There may be several hiring schemes as discussed by Marjit and Beladi (2000). We, however, assume that the unionized sector hires the most efficient ones from amongst $q*$ though that has no implication for the output of this sector. This is not at odds with the reality. We do observe employers picking up workers from the *top* of the efficiency scale, even though that may have little or no bearing on the level or quality of the output they produce. This has often been the screening criterion when jobs are few but job-seekers are large in number.

Given such a hiring-scheme, let us define $\tilde{q} \in \left[q^P, q^* \right]$ such that,

$$q* - \tilde{q} = a_{LY}Y \qquad (9.10)$$

where,

$$Y = \frac{\overline{K} - (\overline{q} - q^*) - \tilde{q}}{a_{KY}} \qquad (9.11)$$

Suppose, $\tilde{q} < q^S$. Thus, by our hiring-scheme, first the graduates are absorbed and then $\left(q^S - \tilde{q} \right)$ number of secondary degree holders is hired, leaving $\tilde{q} - q^P$ number of secondary degree holders to fall back upon the low-skilled export sector. They are unwillingly self-employed getting a lower money return. These are the underemployed people in our model.

We can therefore roughly say that some of the graduates and those having at most primary level of education are self-employed, whereas some of the secondary degree holders are involuntarily self-employed (or underemployed) in the export sector.

9.2.2 Asymmetric Wage Movement Across Skills

In the above scenario we have two measures of wage-inequality at hand given the broad classification of skill. First of all, increase in $[W(q) - \overline{W}]$ is an indicator of growing inequality between graduates self-employed in the export sector and secondary-degree holders working in the unionized import-competing sector. Since the money wage for the latter is fixed, an increase in the money return in the export sector (i.e., $\hat{W}(q) > 0$) implies growing wage inequality between these two classes of workers. But the wage inequality between self-employed graduates and "underemployed" secondary degree holders declines.

On the other hand, $\hat{W}(q)$ is a measure of wage inequality *within* the most-skilled and the least skilled as well as *between* workers belonging to these two classes. In particular, $\hat{W}(q) < 0$ (> 0), i.e., a downward (upward) shift of the wage curve in Figure 9.1, implies an increase (a decline) in wage inequality within and across workers with different education and skill levels. To show this, consider any two workers with abilities or skills $q_1 \in [0, q^P]$, and $q_2 \in [q^*, \tilde{q}]$.

Define $\dfrac{W(q_2)}{W(q_1)}$ as the ratio of their wages. Given our classification of education

and skill levels, this ratio measures the wage-gap or wage-inequality between self-employed graduates and workers with primary degree[32].

Now consider a shift of the $W(q)$-curve, i.e., uniform absolute change in money return for all self-employed workers in the export sector. Denote this shift by α and the (absolute) change in wage ratio by ω. Thus,

$$\omega = \frac{W(q_2) + \alpha}{W(q_1) + \alpha} - \frac{W(q_2)}{W(q_1)} = \frac{\alpha[W(q_1) - W(q_2)]}{W(q_1)[W(q_1) + \alpha]}$$

Since $W_q(q) > 0$ for all q, and $q_1 < q_2$, so $\omega < 0$ if $\alpha > 0$. That is, an upward shift of the $W(q)$-curve, i.e., uniform absolute fall in money return for all self-employed workers in the export sector, implies growing wage inequality among them.

What follows from the above is that an increase (decrease) in money return in the export sector has totally different implications for wage inequality between workers with different education levels and in different occupations. This provides

---

[32] On the other hand, if $q_1, q_2 \in [q^*, \tilde{q}]$ and $q_1 < q_2$, this is a measure of wage inequality within the self-employed graduate workers.

the basis for the observed asymmetric changes in wage inequality among workers of different education and skill levels in India and Chile as pointed out earlier.

Trade liberalization in this set up means a reduction in the ad-valorem tariff and consequently a fall in domestic price of imports. With the money wage in the import-competing sector fixed, the entire burden of such price adjustment is borne by capital. As the rate of return to capital falls, the money wage in the export sector goes up.

Similar result holds when foreign investment is allowed. If initially this small open economy had a high domestic rate of return to capital ($r > r^*$), investment liberalization would lead to inflow of foreign capital depressing the domestic rate of return and consequently raising $W(q)$. Of course, when the domestic return to capital adjusts completely to the given world rate r^*, the unionized sector may not survive with the fixed money wage. However, here what we are interested with is how the wage in the non-unionized sector changes *during* such transition. Thus, whatever be the channel, both trade and investment liberalization raise the money wage in the export sector. Accordingly, as argued above, the wage inequality between self-employed graduates and workers with secondary education working in the import-competing sector widens whereas that between graduates and primary-degree holders declines. This is somewhat similar to what we observe in India during 1988-1994, the period of trade and investment liberalization.

Growing wage inequality in Chile in the late 1970s and early 1980s followed the severe curtailment of union power and lowering of minimum wage following the military overthrow of the Alende Government. One might then wonder whether such regime shift can explain more or less growing but asymmetric wage inequality in Chile in the above theoretical set up.

In the above scenario, given the world commodity prices, lowering of the minimum wage in the import competing sector raises the rate of return to capital and this in turn lowers the money return to workers self-employed in the export sector. This means growing wage inequality among graduates and the primary degree holders. Thus, what appears is that in Chile it is the lowering of the minimum wage, rather than trade liberalization, that explains the changing wage inequality. That is why the inequality between the most and the least educated workers did not go down as in India. On the other hand, letting $\hat{w} < 0$ denote the wage cut, it is straightforward to check that

$$\hat{W}(q) - \hat{w} = \left[\frac{\theta_{LX}}{\theta_{KX}} - 1 \right] \hat{w} \tag{9.12}$$

Therefore, if the import-competing sector is relatively capital-intensive ($\theta_{LY} < \theta_{KY}$), the wage inequality among the self-employed graduates and secondary-degree holders working in the import-competing sector grows following the minimum-wage cut.

9.2.3 Underemployment and Welfare

Given the notion of underemployment, one might be curious about how it may be affected by trade liberalization. Marjit and Beladi (2000) show that underemployment decreases if the factor-substitution elasticity in the unionized sector is sufficiently low. One interesting aspect of the model deserves attention at this point. Consider, for example, the case of Leontief technology in the unionized sector. Under such circumstances, total employment in the unionized sector remains unchanged and underemployment decreases. This happens because with a lower return to capital consequent upon trade liberalization, fewer workers, who would have been *involuntarily* self-employed in the export sector, would now find their present occupation to be profitable and desired. These people, in the post-liberalized state, are no longer underemployed but voluntarily self-employed. These will be the set of workers who are higher up in the skill ladder just below q^*.

In a small country with full employment and no distortions whatsoever, tariff cut is always welfare improving. But here we have wage-distortion and underemployment. How a tariff cut then affects welfare? In presence of unemployment or underemployment, this affects aggregate output. If such effect is adverse, there is a possibility that welfare may fall despite the usual consumption gain that a tariff cut generates.

9.3 Skill Formation and Wage Inequality

Skill formation requires capital and so does the production of skilled and unskilled products. If capital is scarce, at least for the countries which are trying to develop, larger demand for skilled labour has different implications for the left-out unskilled depending on the degree of mobility of capital. This is important for poor countries which may not find conversion of unskilled into skilled an easy proposition. The general equilibrium structure discussed in this section reflects on this problem. In the process we incorporate the assumption that financing human capital formation is expensive relative to financing production of physical output. This assumption lies in the core of an elegant analysis on convergence and growth by Barro and Sala-i-Martin (1991). We capture the essence of this idea by introducing a premium on the return to capital in the skill producing sector vis-à-vis the one where only goods are produced. This again has interesting implications for the skilled-unskilled wage-gap and the absolute wage for the unskilled.

9.3.1 Skill as an Intermediate

Consider an economy which produces two traded final goods, skilled-manufacturing Z and unskilled-manufacturing (or agricultural product) X. Capital is sectorally mobile. At any period the economy is endowed with only unskilled labour and capital. A section of the unskilled workforce is educated or trained as skilled labour. Such human capital or skill formation requires capital and unskilled. The requirement for skilled labour arises as demand for intermediate. Price for skill reflects the foregone wage of a typical unskilled labour and the cost of capital to train up the unskilled :

$$W_S = W + a_{KS} r_S \tag{9.13}$$

Competitive conditions in the goods market imply :

$$P_X = a_{LX}W + a_{KX} r \tag{9.14}$$

$$P_Z = a_{LZ}W_S + a_{KZ} r \tag{9.15}$$

Resources are as usual assumed to be fully employed :

$$\bar{K} = a_{KX}X + a_{KZ}Z + a_{KS}S \tag{9.16}$$

$$\bar{L} = a_{LX}X + S \tag{9.17}$$

$$\bar{S} = a_{SZ}Z \tag{9.18}$$

To capture the imperfect capital market, however, we assume that capital will not flow into the skill producing sector unless is offered a premium :

$$r_S = (1 + \mu) r \tag{9.19}$$

The static nature of the model can be interpreted as a *stationary state* equilibrium. In each period the same number of unskilled workers are available. They acquire skill and then everyone dies at the end of the period. The system repeats itself perpetually. Note that the model displays the typical HOS property. All the factor prices get determined solely by the world prices of the traded goods. Full employment conditions for capital and unskilled labour then determine the output levels of the final traded goods which in turn generate the demand for skilled labour.

Several observations are in order. First, the wage for skilled exceeds the wage for the unskilled by the cost of acquiring human capital which includes a premium (μ) on the rate of return to capital. Competitive market condition in the skill producing sector does not leave any premium for the skilled workers. This is analogous to a similar condition in a typical dynamic model such as Findlay and Kierzkowski (1983). Second, skilled product uses capital directly as well as indirectly through the formation of the skill. We shall assume that good Z to be capital-intensive relative to good X. One implication of such an assumption is that the countries with greater than average endowment of unskilled labour will have, on the average, larger output of unskilled good X, lower output of Z and consequently less skilled people. This directly follows from the application of the Rybczynski theorem discussed in Chapter 3. Larger population implies a smaller absolute number of skilled people.

It is also straightforward to argue that an increase in the relative price of good Z must increase its production and consequently the number of skilled people. Fewer unskilled workers now work towards producing the unskilled good X and get educated instead.

From the Stolper-Samuelson property of the model, the wage-gap widens following such a price increase if skilled-manufacture (Z) is capital-intensive relative to the unskilled-manufacture (X). First of all recall from Chapter 3 that given such an intensity ranking, an increase in P_Z, ceteris paribus, raises the rate of return to capital and reduces the unskilled money wage, both more than proportionately :

$$\hat{r} = \frac{\theta_{LX}}{|\theta|}\hat{P}_Z , \ \hat{W} = -\frac{\theta_{KX}}{|\theta|}\hat{P}_Z \tag{9.20}$$

From (9.12), on the other hand,

$$\hat{W}_S = \theta_{LS}\hat{W} + \theta_{KS}(1+\mu)\hat{r}$$

Subtracting $\hat{W}$ from both sides and using (9.20) this boils down to,

$$\hat{W}_S - \hat{W} = \frac{(1+\mu)\theta_{KS}}{|\theta|}\hat{P}_Z \tag{9.21}$$

Note that higher is the premium μ, greater is the increase in the wage-gap. Higher μ captures greater weight attached to cost of capital in the formation of skill. This is purely due to the premium effect in producing skill. Fairly low value of a_{KS} can be consistent with a very high value of $(1+\mu)\theta_{KS}$. As some skill is required for production of Z, some people get educated, but capital leaves the sector producing X. Due to the standard Stolper-Samuelson argument the existing unskilled workers lose as their wage drops to accommodate for the higher rental. Capital is reallocated for production of skill and Z, thereby widening the wage-gap.

Two points must be noted here. First, if the capital used in production of good X were sector-specific or immobile, an increase in the price of skill-intensive good Z would have actually led to an increase in the unskilled-wage. To see this, suppose K_X is the sector-specific capital required for production of the unskilled labour-intensive good X whereas K_Y is the capital required for production of both skill and the skill-intensive good Z. The economy then behaves essentially as the standard specific-factor model. Replicating the argument in Chapter 3 it is straightforward to check that as P_Z increases, ceteris paribus, the unskilled wage increases too, though less than proportionately. The wage-gap still widens since r_Y, the return to K_Y-type capital used in production of skill, increases (more than proportionate to the increase in P_Z, in fact), but the point to be noted is that unlike the previous case, now the unskilled money wage increases. The inability of capital to leave sector X, in the face of rising returns in the rest of the economy, makes all the difference. Hence, the issue of capital mobility is crucial in the analysis of a price-induced change in skill formation and wage-gap.

Second, the impact of an increase in price of good Z on the wage-gap will be greater for a small economy than for a large economy. Let us think of the initial rise in P_Z/P_X is in consequence of a shift of preference in favour the skill-intensive good Z in the rest-of-the world. The output adjustment in the small economy will not have any feedback effect on the terms of trade. The initial price change is sustained and so is the widening wage-gap. But for the large economy, the increase in production of Z and a decline in production of X would lead to dampening effects on price movements and hence on the wage-gap.

9.3.2 Optimal Skill Formation in an Export Processing Zone

Special economic zones or export processing zones (EPZ), that have been introduced to assume critical role in the development process of many countries, is an institutional arrangement by which certain geographical regions of a country are opened up to foreign investment and technology. Usually, the money wage is at a premium in such zones that attract unskilled labour from hinterland activity. Often foreign technology and investment requires specific skills. Thus the migrating workers need to be trained unless they move with the required skill. In such a context, Marjit and Beladi (1997) demonstrate that if the training cost is increasing in the number of workers migrating into the EPZ, the local government may have a reason to control the inflow of such labour and to maintain an equilibrium wage differential between the EPZ and the hinterland. Such a control has been observed in China where EPZ has played a significant role in its development process.

A slight modification of the above framework captures their idea. Suppose good Z is the export good produced in the EPZ by foreign capital that is perfectly elastic in supply at a given price r^*, and workers drawn from the hinterland. These workers are paid W_S after being trained to attain the specific skill to combine with the foreign capital. The average training cost is assumed to be an increasing function of the total workers in the EPZ :

$$\alpha = \alpha(L_Z), \quad \alpha(0) = 0, \alpha' > 0, \alpha'' > 0 \tag{9.22}$$

As we will show, this increasing cost function is critical for the result. Thus the average labour cost in the EPZ is $W_S + \alpha(L_Z)$. Good X, the import competing good, is produced in the hinterland by unskilled labour and domestic capital. The returns to these factors are W and r respectively.

Since the training cost is borne by the producers in the EPZ (or the workers migrating after acquiring the skill are compensated for such costs), workers migrate from the hinterland till the two wage rates are equalized. In Figure 9.2 this migration equilibrium is shown by the point of intersection between the two curves reflecting the value of marginal product of labour in the EPZ and the hinterland.

But this competitive equilibrium is sub-optimal because the individual migrants only care about W_S but do not internalize the *increase* in the average training cost, $\alpha'(L_Z)$, inflicted upon as they migrate. If one worker is reallocated from the EPZ to the hinterland, the gain from such reallocation are the average training cost, $\alpha'(L_Z^C)L_Z^C$, and the value of marginal product of labour in the hinterland, W^C, whereas the loss is the value of marginal product of labour in the EPZ, W_S^C . Since at the competitive equilibrium, $W_S^C = W^C$, there is a net gain from such reallocation of labour. As we successively labour is withdrawn from the EPZ and put to the hinterland activity, given that the marginal products are diminishing and average training cost is increasing, the net gain falls and the optimal allocation is attained when , $W_S^C = W^C + \alpha'(L_Z^*)$. This is shown in Figure 9.2 by the intersection of the value of marginal product curve for sector-X (VMP$_X$) and AB curve, where the difference between the latter and the value of marginal product curve for sector-Z (VMP$_Z$) curves reflects $\alpha'(L_Z)$. Thus, competitive forces lead to excessive migration to the EPZ and the economy gains by restricting such labour flows.

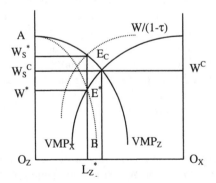

Figure 9.2: Optimal Labour Inflow in EPZ

A simple way to administer this, as suggested by Marjit and Beladi (1997), is to impose a wage-tax in the EPZ. Since at the optimal, wage-differential persists, and individual migrants only care about such difference, the rate of tax equal to $(W_S^* - W^*)$ enforces this optimal allocation.

Interestingly the same story holds when the EPZs are run by foreign capitalists. Larger flow of labour into the EPZs increases return to foreign capital and if that capital income is repatriated, causes a leakage in real national income. Individual workers do not internalize such an outcome and competitive equilibrium leads to excessive allocation of labour into the EPZs. The local government can impose a minimum wage in this sector and the wage-gap is endogenized as a policy decision. Note that a similar result is obtained when the processing zone uses a foreign capital and foreign capital income is repatriated. Even if we do not use the skill formation story there, maximizing national welfare could still mean a wage differential in favour of the processing zone.

9.3.3 Skill as a Product: Role of Fragmentation and Distribution of Capital Stock

In this section we modify the above framework to examine the role initial distribution of capital stock among the individuals. The heterogeneity of agents in terms of their access to capital required for investment in skill formation is the icon of the following exercise. The return from skill is dictated by the amount of capital one puts in. But the skill-based activity has another interpretation also. A product produced through a vertically integrated process requires skill of various types whereas a *fragment* of the process requires a specific skill and hence *lower* investment. Under such circumstances, the agents having substantial capital can hope to earn a lot by investing in, for example, a steel factory, but those with little capital would like to look for markets for fragments. Although this distinction blurs the difference between the cost of acquiring skill and the cost of entrepreneurship, the framework brings home the point we would like to make. We rule out borrowing and lending in the economy primarily because it is a static framework. But a more important assumption is one of capital market imperfection. While investing in skill, contracts cannot be written between the lender and the borrower simply because of the enforceability problem. We can even go further and suggest that with the assumption of economies of scale reflected in the returns to skill, people with larger amount of capital are not likely to lend it out to others. But such an assumption may open the possibility for "buy-outs". We simplify all these by assuming away the existence of an explicit market for credit.

There are three sectors in the economy producing X, Y and S. Good X uses only labour whereas good Y is produced by labour and capital. Good S is actually a skill-based product. We assume that the price of such a product, P_S, is an increasing function of the physical capital invested in such a project. There are two interpretations of this assumption. First, higher investment allows production of better quality product and that sells for higher values. Second, skilled product can be produced as an integrated process. Higher is the initial investment, a longer stretch of the productive spectrum can be completed successfully generating higher values. We also assume that there is a threshold requirement of capital by which we mean that,

$$
\begin{aligned}
P_S &= P_S(k) \quad \forall \; k > \bar{k}_S \\
&= 0 \qquad \forall \; k \le \bar{k}_S
\end{aligned} \tag{9.23}
$$

Of course, for $k > \bar{k}_S$, $P_S'(k) > 0$ and $P_S''(k) < 0$.

There is continuum of agents in this economy indexed by $z \in [0, 1]$ with the population $f(z)$. These agents are ranked in order of their ownership of capital. Thus, if $K(z)$ is the amount of capital owned by the representative agent-z, then $K'(z) > 0$. Note that, if $\bar{L}$ and $\bar{K}$ denote the total labour supply and aggregate stock of capital respectively, then

$$
\bar{L} = \int_0^1 f(z)dz \tag{9.24}
$$

$$
\bar{K} = \int_0^1 K(z)f(z)dz \tag{9.25}
$$

To characterize the poor economy we make the natural assumption that $f'(z) < 0$.

By the competitive conditions we have the usual price equations :

$$
P_X = a_{LX}W \tag{9.26}
$$

$$
P_Y = a_{LY}W + a_{KY}r \tag{9.27}
$$

$$
P_S(K) = a_S W_S(K) \tag{9.28}
$$

With goods X and Y being traded and hence their prices given from outside, the unskilled wage and return to capital are determined from (9.26) and (9.27). The skilled wage or per period return to human capital, on the other hand, is determined from (9.28) given $P_S(K)$ for each value of K.

The allocation of capital between the skilled and unskilled sectors is decided in the following manner. Note that per period return to capital put in to accumulate skill is $W_S(K)$ and to unskilled manufacturing is r. Hence, the maximum capital that will be put in the skilled sector has to be $\tilde{K}$ that satisfies

$$W_S'(\tilde{K}) = r \tag{9.29}$$

Let us also define $\underline{K} < \tilde{K}$ as,

$$W + r\underline{K} = W_S(\underline{K}) \tag{9.30}$$

Then we have the following three groups of population with the income levels defined by $Y_i(z)$, $i = 1, 2, 3$:

$$Y_1(z) = W_S(\tilde{K}) + r\left[K(z) - \tilde{K}\right] \qquad \text{for } K(z) > \tilde{K} \tag{9.31a}$$

$$Y_2(z) = W_S[K(z)] \qquad \text{for } \underline{K} \leq K(z) \leq \tilde{K} \tag{9.31b}$$

$$Y_3(z) = W + rK(z) \qquad \text{for } K(z) < \underline{K} \tag{9.31c}$$

It is also assumed that group 1 supplies only capital to the manufacturing sector. Figure 9.3 shows the possibilities. Therefore,

$$K_Y = \int_0^{\tilde{z}_1} K(z)f(z)dz + \int_{\tilde{z}_2}^1 [K(z) - \tilde{K}]f(z)dz \tag{9.32}$$

where, $z \in [0, \tilde{z}_1]$ and $z \in [\tilde{z}_2, 1]$ denote the groups 1 and 3 that supply capital to the manufacturing sector.

Similarly, supply of labour available for sectors X and Y is given by,

$$L_X + L_Y = \int_0^{\tilde{z}_1} f(z)dz \tag{9.33}$$

It is now straightforward to solve for X and Y from the following conditions :

$$L_X + L_Y = a_{LX}X + a_{LY}Y \tag{9.34}$$

$$K_Y = a_{LY}Y \tag{9.35}$$

Of course, we can guarantee positive output levels only when factor intensities are such that,

$$\frac{a_{LX}}{a_{KX}} > \frac{L_X + L_Y}{K_Y} > \frac{a_{LY}}{a_{KY}} \tag{9.36}$$

Since in our formulation $a_{KX} = 0$ and $K_Y > 0$, so the left-hand-side inequality in (9.32) is satisfied. We assume that the right-hand-side inequality holds. That is, we assume that the factor endowment line is within the cone of diversification defined by the factor intensities so that both these goods are produced together with the skilled product.

Note that the poorest cannot afford to invest in skill and some of the not-so-poor (with $K_S < K(t) < \underline{K}$ choose not to do so. Then the middle ones go all out for skill whereas the rich ones partly invest in skill and partly in the unskilled manufacturing.

Let us provide two examples in terms of comparative static that alters the pattern of income distribution and skill formation. We assume the following trade pattern for the economy under consideration. Good X is a traditional exportable and Y is an importable, whereas S represents a new set of exported goods.

Suppose that the price of traditional export good X increases because freer trade opens up the possibility of exporting more of this good. This immediately raises the wage rate and reduces the rate of return to capital. Accordingly $\tilde{K}$ increases which in turn increases the allocation of capital towards skill formation. Some of the rich will put their entire capital for skill formation. Some of the not-so-poor will move towards acquiring skill. Capital flows back to skill formation, production of the import-competing good contracts and unskilled labour are released towards the export production.

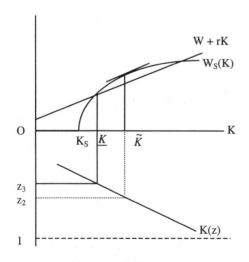

Figure 9.3: Decision of Skill Formation

Let us look at $Y_1(z)/Y_3(z)$ for those in group-3 who stay back in their group. It can be easily checked that the sign of $d[Y_1(z)/Y_3(z)]$ depends on the sign of $[Y_1(z)-Y_3(z)]K(z)dr - \tilde{K} dr - Y_1(z)dW$. Note that higher unskilled money wage improves the income of the poorest and, hence, implies reduction in inequality. If the rate of return to capital goes down, $\tilde{K}$ goes up and the rich gains due to better returns from skill. This tends to worsen the inequality as captured by the second term. But a drop in rate of return to capital reduces the capital income and as $Y_1(z) - Y_3(z)$, it hurts the rich and thereby leads to a possible decline in inequality as captured by the first term. The interesting point to note is that a rise in unskilled-wage can increase skill formation and reduce inequality at the same time by lowering the return to capital.

Our second example concerns greater integration of the global markets and revolution in information technology. These can increase the skilled wage, $W_S(K)$, for each level of capital. However, we can contemplate that in some cases such benefits from skill formation can be reaped only for higher levels of capital. In that case clearly the degree of inequality will increase since unskilled money wage and return to capital remain unaffected but   increases for relatively high value of capital. On the other hand, the $W_S(K)$ function in Figure 9.3 can shift that helps poor and middle class people, thus bringing about a more egalitarian change.
Indeed, what we sketch as examples, can easily be demonstrated in a full blown model.

9.4 Conclusion

In this chapter we have focused on two particular issues. First is the asymmetric impact of trade and investment liberalization on wage inequality across different skills as has been observed in India and partly in Chile. This aspect of widening wage-gap phenomenon has received little theoretical attention so far.

The other issue that has been analyzed is that of skill formation. In the discussion of widening wage-gap, skill has been taken as something exogenously given. But an overpowering consequence of globalization for the developing countries is its impact on the internal demand for and supply of skill. Increasing trade and investment requires specialized skills which may be in short supply in a developing country. Hence one would expect that with the expansion of trade, the process of skill formation would also get a natural boost increasing the knowledge base of the economy which in turn will have growth enhancing effects. We have discussed this process of skill formation in two alternative scenarios. When the decision of acquiring skill involves a choice for the unskilled between putting her initial endowment of capital into production of final good and into the skilled activity, it is, of course, quite possible that an increase in price of the traditional exports induces people with very small endowment as well those with very large endowment of capital to invest in skill. A decline in the price of the import good, on the other hand, unambiguously expands the set of skilled people. Moreover, with the consequent increase in the wage-rental ratio, the income distribution moves in favour of the poor.

10 CONCLUSION

The phenomenon of growing wage inequality across the world during the 1980s and 1990s has posed quite a few challenges to the economists. Foremost is to clearly distinguish the roles of more open-minded trade policies and technological changes as dominant factors behind such outcomes. Second, if trade is the main cause, how to explain the widening wage-gap both in the North and in the South. The latter has been the major concern for the trade theorists primarily because the existing theories and models of trade fail to establish such a nexus between freer trade and wage inequality. As is discussed in Chapter 3, if one goes by the standard HOS model, freer trade can at best lead to asymmetric wage movements in the North and the South. Moreover, South being relatively abundant in unskilled-labour, should experience an increase in the relative wage for its unskilled workers. Thus, if one has to argue in favour of trade causing wage inequality, the first task at hand would be to establish the observed relationship at the theoretical level.

In this book we have taken up this challenge. We have provided a plethora of models within the ambit of general equilibrium framework that capture the changing nature of the North-South trade relations and structural features of trade and production patterns that distinguish the South from the North.

In Chapters 4 and 5, we have talked about two possible channels through which trade liberalization leads to widening wage-gap in both the North and the South. First is the multi-commodity HOS model where the endowments of the countries are so dissimilar that they produce in common only the middle-good in terms of the intensity ranking. If North is a net importer of this good and lowers its initial tariff on it, the consequent wage-movements are indeed symmetric. Second is the case of input trade between the North and the South that is now the order of the day [see Feenstra and Hanson (2001)]. A simple extension of the specific-factor model to incorporate such a phenomenon provides another basis for trade widening the wage-gap. Of course, inflow of capital from the North to the South might also cause this, but this does not seem to be theoretically obvious.

Unskilled workers in Europe and in some parts of Asia have been hit by trade liberalization in a different way. With money wage being determined through bargaining with the trade unions, the deteriorating position of them has been felt through a loss of employment. Chapter 6 has discussed at length how the dual-economy and general equilibrium models, when modified properly, can shed lights on such contractionary effects of trade and investment liberalization.

In Part IV we have been primarily concerned with developing simple general equilibrium models for the South taking into account some of its specific production, trade and market structures. The purpose has been to examine whether such structural features can contribute to the trade-inequality nexus. A good number of developing countries are now exporting skill-intensive manufacturing goods like software besides their traditional unskilled-labour intensive agricultural goods. Once such diversified trade pattern is recognized and taken into the analysis, freer trade causing greater wage inequality in the South may not seem to be a puzzling one. But what we have demonstrated in Chapter 7 is that even agricultural trade liberalization, that pushes up the price of agricultural goods and the money wage for the unskilled workers, may raise wage inequality. This happens because there is a latent complementarity between manufacturing and agricultural exports through which skilled money wage increases as well. Trade in fragments is another channel through which wage inequality might grow in the South.

Coexistence of formal and informal sectors is a typical feature of many developing countries. Globalization has been observed to reduce the size of the formal sector and expand that of the informal sector. Since informal wages are usually low and determined by the market forces, one is tempted to conclude that such informalization by itself contributes to the deteriorating position of the unskilled workers in absolute as well as relative terms. Chapter 8 finds that such an apprehension is not a foregone conclusion. Much depends on whether capital can also move out of the contracting formal sector along with the unskilled labour. If it can, money wage will in fact increase. Thus, effect of informalization on the unskilled workers essentially depends on the specificity and mobility of capital.

The production of non-traded good is another plausible explanation for growing wage inequality in the South. The more important issue, however, is the nature of such non-traded production. When such non-traded good is produced in the informal segment of the economy, the degree of wage inequality changes compared to the case of formal-sector production of the non-traded good.

In the final chapter, we have taken up two issues. Attempt has been made to provide a simple theoretical explanation for the asymmetric movements of relative wages among workers with varying levels of educational and skill, that have been observed in Chile and in India. We also have explored how far trade induced skill formation can contribute towards growing wage inequality. However, this is the area where further work is needed to be done.

We have some workable theoretical models and plausible results at hand which should energize empirical testability of the trade-wage inequality hypothesis. What we have identified here are the avenues through which trade and investment can impact on wage inequality. Isolating the exact effects and identifying whether they work through diversified trade pattern, fragmentation, input trade, informalization or skill formation, however, are fundamentally empirical questions and seem to be open-ended from our point of view. However, we can assert with conviction that well grounded general equilibrium models of trade and production should be the main work-horse if one is keen on acquiring a deeper understanding of the problem of trade and wage inequality.

LIST OF FIGURES

LIST OF TABLES

BIBLIOGRAPHY

Acemoglu, D. (1999): Changes in Unemployment and Wage Inequality: An Alternative Theory and Some Evidence. American Economic Review, December, 1259- 1278.

Acharyya, R. (1994a): Liberalized Exchange Rate Management System and Devaluation in India: Trade Balance Effect. Journal of Economic Integration , 9(4), 534-42.

Acharyya, R. (1994b): Principle of Effective Demand and the Vent for Surplus Approach to Trade. Journal of Post Keynesian Economics, Spring, 16(3), 439-451.

Acharyya, R., and S. Marjit (1998): Devaluation and Employment. A Brief Survey and Some New Results. In: B. Chatterjee (Ed.): Economic Liberalization in India. Allied Publishers, Calcutta.

Acharyya, R., and S. Marjit (1999): Trade Liberalization and Wage-Gap in the Developing Countries. The Role of the Informal Non-Traded Sector. Working Paper 112, The Chinese University of Hong Kong.

Acharyya, R., and S. Marjit (2000a): Trade, Labour and Wage Inequality in the Developing Nations. A Simple General Equilibrium Approach. Mimeo, Jadavpur University.

Acharyya, R., and S. Marjit (2000b): Globalization and Inequality. Towards an Analytical Perspective. Economic and Political Weekly,Vol. XXXV, No. 39 (Sept. 23-29).

Acharyya, R., and S. Marjit (2001): Trade Liberalization and Wage Inequality Among Skill-Differentiated Workers. Mimeo, Jadavpur University.

Acharyya, R.. (2002): Globalization, Rigged Rules and Double Standards. A Review of Oxfam Report 2002. Decision 29 (3/4). Calcutta: Indian Institute of Management.

Agenor, P.R. (1996): The Labour Market and Economic Adjustment. IMF Staff Paper 32, 261-335.

Agenor, P.R., and P. Montiel (1996): Development Macroeconomics. Princeton University Press, Princeton.

Aryytey, A., H. Hettige, M. Nissanke and W. Heel (1997): Financial Market Fragmentation and Reforms in Ghana, Malwai, Nigeria and Tanzania. World Bank Economic Review 11, 195-218.

Banerjee, A.V., and A. Newman (1993): Occupational Choice and the Process of Development. Journal of Political Economy 101, 274-98.

Barro, R. J., and X. Sala-i-Martin (1991): Convergence Across States and Regions. Brookings Papers on Economic Activity 1 , 107-82.

Beladi, H., and S. Marjit (1992): Foreign Capital and Protection. Canadian Journal of Economics 25, 233-38.

Beladi, H., and S. Marjit (1996): An analysis of Rural-Urban Migration and protection. Canadian Journal of Economics 29, 930-40.

Beladi, H., and S. Marjit (1999): Foreign Capital Inflows, the Non-Traded Sector and welfare. Development Policy Review 17, 79-84.

Beladi, H., and S. Marjit, and R. Frasca (1998): Foreign Capital Accumulation and National Income. Does Unemployment Matter? Keio Economic Studies 35, 19-27.

Berman, E., J. Bound and Z. Grilliches (1994): Changes in the Demand for Skilled Labour Within U.S. Manufacturing Industries. Quarterly Journal of Economics 104, 367-398.

Bernard, A.B., and J.B. Jensen (1997): Exporters, Skill Upgrading and the Wage Gap. Journal of International Economics 42, 3-32.

Beyer, H., P. Rojas, and R. Vergara (1999): Trade Liberalization and Wage Inequality. Journal of Development Economics 59, 103-23.

Bhaduri, A. (1986): Macroeconomics: The Dynamics of Commodity Production. M.E. Sharpe, Armonk, New York.

Bhagwati, J.N. (1991): Free Traders and Free Immigrationists. Strangers or friends? Russell Sage Foundation, New York. Working Paper 20.

Bhagwati, J.N. (1995): Trade and Wages. A Malign Relationship? Unpublished Manuscript, Columbia University.

Bhagwati, J.N., and V.H. Dahejia (1998): Free Trade and Wages of the Unskilled: Is Marx Striking Again? In: V.N. Balasubramanyam (Ed.): J.N Bhagwati, Writings on International Economics, Oxford University Press, Delhi.

Bhagwati, J.N., and V.K. Ramaswami (1963): Domestic Distortions, Tariffs and the Theory of Optimum Subsidy. Journal of Political Economy 71, 44-50.

Bhalla, S. (1997): The Rise and Fall of Workforce Diversification Processes in Rural India". In: G.K. Chadha and A.N. Sharma (Eds.): Growth, Employment and Poverty in Rural India. Vikas Publishing House, Delhi.

Borjas, G.J., Freeman, R.B., and L.F. Katz (1992): On the Labour Market Effects of Immigration and Trade. In: Borjas, G. J., and R. B. Freeman (Eds.): Immigration and the Work Force. University of Chicago Press, Chicago.

Bose, A. (1989): Short Period Equilibrium in a Less Developed Economy. In: M.K. Rakshit (Ed.): Studies in Macroeconomics of Developing Countries. Oxford University Press, Delhi.

Bound, J. and G. Johnson (1992): Changes in the Structure of Wages in the 1980s: An Evaluation of Alternative Explanations. American Economic Review 82, 371-92.

Brecher, R. (1974): Minimum Wage Rates and the Pure Theory of International Trade. Quarterly Journal of Economics 88, 98-116.

Buffie, E.F. (1984): The Macroeconomics of Trade Liberalization. Journal of International Economics 17, 121-37.

Caves, R.E., J.A. Frankel, and R.W. Jones (1997): World Trade and Payments. An Introduction, Seventh Edition. Harper Collins.

Chakrabarti, A. (2001): Do Nations that Trade More Have a More Unequal Distribution of Income? Mimeo, University of Wisconsin-Milwaukee.

Chao, Chi-Chur, and E. Yu (1993): Content Protection, Urban Unemployment and Welfare. Canadian Journal of Economics 26, 481-92.

Cole, W.E. and R.D. Sanders (1985): Internal Migration and Urban Employment in the Third World. American Economic Review 75, 481-94.

Cooper, R.N. (1971): Devaluation and Aggregate Demand in Aid-Receiving Countries. In : J.N. Bhagwati et. al. (Eds.): Trade, Balance of Payments and Growth. North Holland, Amsterdam.

Das, S.P. (2001): Trade and Personal Income Distribution. Pacific Economic Review 6, 1-24.

Davis, D. (1996): Trade Liberalization and Income Distribution. NBER Working Paper No. 5693.

Davis, D. (1998): Does European Unemployment Prop Up American Wages? National Labour Markets and Global Trade. American Economic Review.

Deardorff, A. (1984): Testing Trade Theories and Predicting Trade Flows. In: Jones, R.W. and P. Kenen (Eds.): Handbook of International Economics, Vol. 1. North Holland, Amsterdam.

Deardorff, A. (2000): Factor Prices and the Factor Content of Trade Revisited : What's the Use? Journal of International Economics 50, 73-90.

Deardorff, A., and D. Hakura (1994) : Trade and Wages : What are the Questions? In: Bhagwati, J.N., and M. Kosters (Eds.): Trade and Wages: Leveling Wages Down. American Enterprise Institute, Washington.

Deardorff, A., and R. Staiger (1988): An Interpretation of Factor Content of Trade. Journal of International Economics 24 , 93-107.

Dev, M. (2000) : Economic Liberalization and Employment in South Asia. Economic and Political Weekly, January.

Diaz-Alejandro, C.F. (1963): A Note on the Impact of Devaluation and the Redistributive Effect. Journal of Political Economy (December), 577-80.

Dornbusch, R. (1980): Open Economy Macroeconomy. Basic Books, NY.

Dornbusch, R., S. Fisher, and P. Samuelson (1977): Comparative Advantage, Trade and Payments in a Ricardian Model With Continuum of Goods. American Economic Review 47, 823-39.

Dutt, R. (1994): New Economic Policy: A Review. The Indian Journal of Labour Economics 37, 203-14.

Edwards, S. (1997) : Trade Policy, Growth, and Income Distribution. American Economic Review 87(2), 205-10.

Edwards, A.C., and Sebastian Edwards (1995): Trade Liberalization and Unemployment: Evidences from Chile. University of California, Los Angeles.

Feenstra, R., and G. Hanson (1996): Foreign Investment, Outsourcing and Relative Wages. In: R. Feenstra, G. Grossman and D. Irwin (Eds): Political Economy of Trade Policies. Essays in Honour of J.N. Bhagwati. MIT Press, MA.

Feenstra, R., and G. Hanson (2001): Global Production and Rising Inequality: A Survey of Trade and Wages. NBER Working Paper.

Fields, G. (1990): Labour Market Modeling and the Urban Informal Sector: Theory and Evidence. In : Turnham, D. (Ed.): The Informal Sector and Evidence Revisited. OECD, Paris.

Findlay, R. (1984): Growth and Development in Trade Models. In : Jones, R.W., and P. Kenen (Eds.) : Handbook of International Economics, Vol. I. North Holland, Amsterdam.

Findlay, R. (1995): Factor Proportions, Trade and Growth. MIT Press, MA.

Findlay, R., and H. Kierzkowski (1983): International Trade and Human Capital: A Simple General Equilibrium Model. Journal of Political Economy 91, 957-78.

Freeman, R., and L. Katz (1994): Rising Wage Inequality: The United States vs. Other Advanced Countries. In R. Freeman (Ed.) : Working Under Different Rules. Russell Sage Foundation, NY.

Gal-or, O. and J. Zeira (1993) : Income Distribution and Macroeconomics. Review of Economic Studies 60, 35-52.

Gupta, M.R. (1994) : Foreign Capital, Income Inequality and Welfare in a Harris-Todaro model. Journal of Development Economics 45, 407-414.

Gupta, M.R. (1995): Tax on Foreign Capital Income and Wage Subsidy to the Urban Sector in the Harris-Todaro Model. Journal of Development Economics 47(2), 469-79.

Gupta, M.R. (1997): Informal Sector and Informal Capital Market in a Small Open Less Developed Economy. Journal of Development Economics 52 (2), 409-28.

Gruen, F.H. and W. M. Corden (1970) : A Tariff that Worsens the Terms of Trade. In : I.A. McDougall and R.H. Snape (Eds.) : Studies in International Economics. North Holland, Amsterdam.

Haberler, G. (1950) : Some Problems in the Pure Theory of International Trade. Economic Journal LX (June), 223-40.

Harris, R.G. (1993): Globalization, Trade and Income. Canadian Journal of Economics, November.

Harris, R.G. (1995): Trade and Communication Costs. Canadian Journal of Economics, November.

Hazari, B., and Sgro, P. (1991): Urban-Rural Structural Adjustment and Urban Unemployment with Traded and Non-Traded Goods. Journal of Development Economics 35, 187-96.

Hazari, B., Jayasuriya, S. and Sgro, P. (1992): Tariffs, Terms of Trade, Unemployment and the Real Exchange Rate. Southern Economic Journal (January), 721-31.

Helpman, E. (1976): Macroeconomic Policy in a Model of International Trade With a Wage Restriction. International Economic Review June, 262-77.

Johnson, H.G. (1965): Optimal Trade Intervention in Presence of Domestic Distortions. In : R.E. Baldwin et. al. (Eds.) : Trade, Growth and Balance of Payments. Essays in Honour of G. Haberler. North Holland, Amsterdam.

Jones, R.W. (1965): The Structure of Simple General Equilibrium Models. Journal of Political Economy 73, 557-72.

Jones, R.W. (1967) : International Capital Movements and the Theory of Tariffs and Trade. Quarterly Journal of Economics, February, 1-38.

Jones, R.W. (1971): A Three Factor Model in Trade, Theory and History. In : J.N. Bhagwati et. al. (Eds.): Trade, Balance of Payments and Growth. North Holland, Amsterdam.

Jones, R.W. (1979): International Trade. Essays in Theory. North Holland, Amsterdam.

Jones, R.W. (2001): Globalization and Theory of Input Trade. MIT Press, MA.

Jones, R.W., H. Beladi and S. Marjit (1999): Three Faces of Factor Intensities. Journal of International Economics 48, 413-20.

Jones, R.W. and M. Corden (1976): Devaluation, Non-Flexible Prices and Trade Balance for a Small Country. Canadian Journal of Economics 9, 150-61.

Jones, R.W. and S.L. Engerman (1996): Trade, Technology and Wages. A Tale of Two Countries. American Economic Review 86, 35-40.

Jones, R.W. and H. Kierzkowski (1990): The Role of Services in Production and International Trade: A Theoretical Framework. In : R.W. Jones and A. Krueger (Eds.) : The Political Economy of International Trade. Basil Blackwell, Oxford.

Jones, R.W. and H. Kierzkowski (2001a): Globalization and the Consequences of International Fragmentation. In: G. Calvo, R. Dornbusch, and M. Obstfeld (Eds.):

Money, Capital Mobility and Trade. Essays in Honour of Robert A. Mundell. MIT Press, MA.

Jones, R.W. and H. Kierzkowski (2001b): A Framework for Fragmentation. In : Sven Arndt and H. Kierzkowski (Eds.): Fragmentation. New Production Patterns in the World Economy. Oxford University Press, Clarendon.

Jones, R.W. and S. Marjit (1992): International Trade and Endogenous Production Structures. In : R. Riezman and W. Neuefiend (Eds.) : Economic Theory and International Trade. Springer-Verlag.

Jones, R.W. and S. Marjit (2001a): The Role of International Fragmentation in the Development Process. American Economic Review, May.

Jones, R.W. and S. Marjit (2001b): Economic Development, Trade and Wages. Mimeo, University of Rochester.

Kalecki, M. (1937): The Problem of Effective Demand with Tugan Baranovski and Rosa Luxemburg. Reprinted in: M. Kalecki (1971): Selected Essays on the Dynamics of Capitalist Economy. Cambridge University Press, Cambridge.

Katz, L. and D. Autor (1999): Changes in Wage Structure and Earnings Inequality. In : O. Ashenfelter and D. Card (Eds.) : Handbook of Labour Economics, Vol. 3A. North Holland, Amsterdam.

Katz, L., G.W. Loveman and D.G. Blanchflower (1992): A Comparison of Changes in the Structure of Wages in Four OECD Countries. NBER.

Katz, L. and K. Murphy (1992): Changes in Relative Wages, 1963 – 1987. Supply and Demand Factors. Quarterly Journal of Economics CVII, 36 – 78.

Kemp, M. (1966): The Gain From International Trade and Investment: A Neo-Heckscher-Ohlin Approach. American Economic Review, September.

Khan, M.A. (1980): The Harris-Todaro Hypothesis and the Heckscher-Ohlin-Samuelson Model. A Synthesis. Journal of International Economics 10, 527-47.

Khan, M.A. (1982): Tariffs, Foreign Capital and Immiserizing Growth with Urban Unemployment and Specific-Factors of Production. Journal of Development Economics 10, 245-56.

Khan, A.R. (1998a): The Impact of Globalization in South Asia. In : A.S. Bhalla (Ed.) : Globalization, Growth and Marginalization. Macmillan.

Khan, A.R. (1998b): Growth and Poverty in East and South-East Asia in the Era of Globalization. In: A.S. Bhalla (Ed.): Globalization, Growth and Marginalization. Macmillan.

Krugman, P. (1995): Growing World Trade: Causes and Consequences. Brookings Papers on Economic Activity 1, 327-62.

Krugman, P.R. (2000): Technology, Trade and Factor Prices. Journal of International Economics 50, 51-71.

Krugman, P. and L. Taylor (1978) : Contractionary Effects of Devaluation. Journal of International Economics, 445-56.

Lall, S. (2001): The Technological Structure and Performance of Developing Country Manufactured Exports, 1985-1998. Oxford Development Studies, 28(3).

Lawrence, R.Z. (1994): Trade, Multinationals and Labour. NBER Working Paper 4836.

Lawrence, R.Z. and M.J. Slaughter (1993) : International Trade and American Wages in the 1980s. Giant Sucking Sound or Small Hiccup?. Brookings Papers on Economic Activity. Microeconomics, 161-226.

Leamer, E. (1995): A Trade Economists's View of US Wages and Globalization. In: S. M. Collins (Ed.): Imports, Exports and the American Worker. Brookings Institution Press, Washington DC.

Leamer, E. (1998): In Search of Stolper-Samuelson Linkages Between International Trade and Lower Wages. S. M. Collins (Ed.) : Imports, Exports and the American Worker. Brookings Institution Press, Washington DC.

Leamer, E. (2000): What's the Use of Factor Contents? Journal of International Economics 50, 51-71.

Leontief, W.W. (1956): Factor Proportions and the Structure of American Trade. Further Theoretical and Empirical Analysis. Review of Economics and Statistics 38, 386-407.

Mallik, A. (1977): A Note on Multiplier and Real Wage Adjustment. Indian Statistical Institute Technical Report No. ERU/2/27.

Marjit, S. (1990): A Simple Production Model in Trade and Its Applications. Economics Letters.

Marjit, S. (1997): Terms of Trade and Wage Gap in Developing Countries. Mimeo, Centre for Studies in Social Sciences, Calcutta.

Marjit, S. (1999): Trade, Wage Inequality and the Developing Nations. Mimeo, Centre for Studies in Social Sciences, Calcutta.

Marjit, S. (2000): Economic Reform and Informalization in a Developing Economy. A General Equilibrium Analysis. DSA Working Paper 15/2000, Jawaharlal Nehru University.

Marjit, S. and H. Beladi (1997a): An Analysis of Optimal Size for a Special Economic Zone. Swiss Journal of Economics and Statistics 133, 153-64.

Marjit, S. and H. Beladi (1997b) : Protection and Gainful Effects of Foreign Capital. Economics Letters 53, 311-26.

Marjit, S. and H. Beladi (1998): Trade and Wage Inequality in Developing Countries. Mimeo, Centre for Studies in Social Sciences, Calcutta.

Marjit, S., and H. Beladi (1999): Complementarity Between Import Competition and Import Promotion. Journal of Economic Theory 86, 280-85.

Marjit, S. and H. Beladi (2000): Protection, Underemployment and Welfare. EPRU, Copenhagen Business School Working Paper.

Marjit, S. and H. Beladi (2002): The Stolper-Samuelson Theorem in a Wage-Differential Framework. Forthcoming in The Japanese Economic Review.

Marjit, S., U. Broll and S. Mitra (1997): Targeting Sectors for Foreign Capital Inflow in a Small Developing Economy. Review of International Economics 5, 101-06.

Marjit, S., U. Broll and S. Sengupta (2000): Trade and Wage-Gap in Poor Countries. The Role of the Informal Sector. In: A. Bose et. al. (Eds.): Macro, Trade and Institutions. Essays in Honour of M.K. Rakshit. Oxford University Press, Delhi.

Markusen, J.R. and A.J. Venables (1996): The Role of Multinational Firms in the Wage-Gap Debate. NBER Working Paper 5483.

Mayer, W. (1974) : Short-Run and Long-Run Equilibrium for a Small Open Economy. Journal of Political Economy 82, 955 – 968.

Mayer, J. and A. Wood (2000): South Asia's Export Structure in a Comparative Perspective. IDS Working Paper 91. Institute for Development Studies, Sussex.

Mazumdar, D. (1983): Segmented Labour Markets in LDCs. American Economic Review 73, 254-59.

Mazumdar, D. (1993): Labour Markets and Adjustment in Open Asian Economies. The Republic of Korea and Malaysia. World Bank Economic Review 7, 349-80.

Meller, P. (1998): Trade and Employment in Latin America. In: O. Memedovic et. al. (Eds.): Globalization of Labour Markets. Challenges, Adjustments and Policy Response in the European Union and Less Developed Countries. Kluwer Academic Publishers.

Michaely, M., Papageorgiou, D. and A.M. Choksi (1991): Lessons and Experiences in the Developing World. Basil Blackwell, Oxford.

Mundell, R. (1957): International Trade and Factor Mobility. American Economic Review 47, 321-35.

Murphy, K.M. and F. Welch (1991): The Role of International Trade in Wage Differentials. In: M. Kosters (Ed.): Workers and Their Wages. Changing Pattern in the United States. The American Enterprise, Washington.

Mussa, M. (1974): Tariffs and the Distribution of Income. The Importance of Factor Specificity, Substitutability and Intensity in the Short and Long Run. Journal of Political Economy 82, 1191 – 1204.

Noman, K. and R.W. Jones (1979): A Model of Trade and Unemployment. In J.R. Green and J.A. Sheinkman (Eds.) : General Equilibrium, Growth and Trade. Essays in Honour of L. McKenzie. Academic Press, New York.

Oxfam (2002): Rigged Rules and Double Standards. Trade, Globalization and Fight Against Poverty. Oxfam International, Washington.

Panagariya, A. (2000): Evaluating the Factor-Content Approach to Measuring the Effect of Trade on Wage Inequality. Journal of International Economics 50, 51-71.

Pedersen, K. (1998): Comment on Trade and Employment in Latin America. In: O. Memedovic et. al. (Eds.): Globalization of Labour Markets. Challenges, Adjustments and Policy Response in the European Union and Less Developed Countries. Kluwer Academic Publishers.

Rakshit, M. (1982): The Labour Surplus Economy. Macmillan, Delhi and Humanities Press, New Jersey.

Rao, M. (1999): Openness, Poverty and Inequality. Background Papers, Human Development Report. UNDP.

Reich, R.B. (1991): The Work of Nations. Alfred A. Knopf, New York.

Robbins, D. (1994a): Malaysian Wage Structure and Its Causes. Working Paper, Harvard Institute for International Development.

Robbins, D. (1994b): Philippine Wage and Employment Structure. Working Paper, Harvard Institute for International Development.

Robbins, D. (1995a): Earnings Dispersion in Chile After Trade Liberalization. Working Paper, Harvard Institute for International Development.

Robbins, D. (1995b): Trade, Trade Liberalization and Inequality in Latin America and East Asia. Synthesis of Seven Country Studies. Working Paper, Harvard Institute of International Development.

Robbins, D. (1996a) : Stolper-Samuelson Lost in the Topics. Trade Liberalization and Wages in Columbia. Working Paper, Harvard Institute of International Development.

Robbins, D. (1996b): HOS Hits Facts: Facts Win. Evidence on Trade and Wages in Developing World. Working Paper, Harvard Institute of International Development.

Robbins, D. and T. Zveglich (1995): Skill-Bias in Recent Taiwanese Growth. Working Paper, Harvard Institute of International Development.

Rodas-Martini, P. (1999): Income Inequality Within and Between Countries. Main Issues in the Literature. Background Papers, Human Development Report. UNDP.

Rodrigo, C. (1988): Employment, Wages and Income Distribution in Sri Lanka. ILO/ARTEP, New Delhi.

Salter, W.E. (1959): Internal and External Balance. The Role of Price and Expenditure Effects. Economic Record 35, 226-38.

Samuelson, P. (1948): International Trade and the Equalization of Factor Prices. Economic Journal 58, 163-84.

Sanyal, K. K. and R. W. Jones (1982): The Theory of Trade in Middle Products. American Economic Review, March.

Shariff, A. and A. Gumber (1999): Employment and Wages in India. Pre and post Reforms. Indian Journal of Labour Economics 42, 195-216.

Slaughter, M.J. (1995): Multinational Corporations, Outsourcing and the American Relative Wage Divergence. NBER Working Paper 5253.

Spencer, B. and R.W. Jones (1991): Vertical Foreclosure and International Trade Policy. Review of Economic Studies, January, 153-70.

Spencer, B. and R.W. Jones (1992): Trade and Protection in Vertically Related Markets. Journal of International Economics, February.

Stolper, W.F. and P. Samuelson (1941): Protection and Real Wages. Review of Economic Studies, November, 51-68.

Swan, T. (1960): Economic Control in a Dependent Economy. Economic Record 36, 51-66.

Taylor, Lance (1983): Structuralist Macroeconomics. Basic Books, New York.

Tendulkar, S., Sundaram D.K. and L.R. Jain (1996): Macroeconomic Policies and Poverty in India 1966-67 to 1993-94. Manuscript. ILO, New Delhi.

Torvik, R. (1994): Trade Policy Under a Binding Foreign Exchange Constraint. Journal of International Trade and Development, March, 15-31.

Trefler, D. (1993): International Factor Price Differences. Leontief Was Right! Journal of Political Economy 101, 961 – 987.

Vanek, J. (1968): The Factor Proportions Theory. The N-Factor Cases. Kyklos 21, 749 – 756.

Wong, Kar-Yiu (1995): International Trade in Goods and Factor Mobility. MIT Press, MA.

Wong, Siu-kee (1998): Essays on Tariffs, Trade and Factor Mobility. Unpublished Ph.D. dissertation, University of Rochester.

Wood, A. (1994): North-South Trade, Employment and Inequality. Changing Fortunes in a Skill-Driven World. Clarendon Press, Oxford.

Wood, A. (1997) : Openness and Wage Inequality in Developing Countries. The Latin American Challenge to East Asian Conventional Wisdom. World Bank Research Observer 11(1), 33-57.

Wood, A. and M. Calandrino (2001): When Other Giants Awakens. Trade and Human Resources in India. Economic and Political Weekly, XXXV, 4677-94.

INDEX